· THE TANNER LECTURES IN MORAL PHILOSOPHY

TAKING OURSELVES SERIOUSLY

———————————

GETTING IT RIGHT

Taking Ourselves Seriously

&

Getting It Right

Harry G. Frankfurt

Edited by Debra Satz

With Comments by Christine M. Korsgaard,
Michael E. Bratman, and Meir Dan-Cohen

Stanford University Press
2006

Stanford University Press
Stanford, California
© 2006 by the Board of Trustees of the Leland Stanford Junior University.
All rights reserved.

Printed in the United States of America on acid-free, archival-quality paper

LIBRARY OF CONGRESS CATALOGING-IN-PUBLICATION DATA

Frankfurt, Harry G., 1929–
Taking ourselves seriously and getting it right / Harry G. Frankfurt ;
edited by Debra Satz.
p.   cm.
Includes bibliographical references and index.
ISBN-13: 978-0-8047-5298-5 (pbk. : alk. paper)
1. Conduct of life. 2. Love. 3. Reflection (Philosophy) 4. Self.
I. Satz, Debra. II. Title.
BJ1531.F73   2006
170—dc22   006017978

Designed by Rob Ehle and set in 12/16 Seria.

170
FR

Contents

Contributors

HARRY G. FRANKFURT is professor emeritus at Princeton University. His books include *Demons, Dreamers, and Madmen: The Defense of Reason in Descartes's Meditations* (1970), *The Importance of What We Care About: Philosophical Essays* (1988), *Necessity, Volition, and Love* (1999), *The Reasons of Love* (2004), and *On Bullshit* (2005). He has written more than 50 scholarly articles, essays, and reviews.

MICHAEL E. BRATMAN is the Durfee Professor in the School of Humanities & Sciences and professor of philosophy at Stanford University. He is the author of *Intention, Plans, and Practical Reason* (1987) and *Faces of Invention: Selected Essays on Intention and Agency* (1999). His book of essay *Structures of Agency* will be published in 2007.

MEIR DAN-COHEN is the Milo Reese Robbins Chair in Legal Ethics at Boalt Hall School of Law, University of California at Berkeley. He is the author of *Rights, Persons, and*

Organizations: A Legal Theory for Bureaucratic Society (1986), and
Harmful Thoughts: Essays on Law, Self, and Morality (2002). He
has published a number of articles in criminal law and in
legal and moral philosophy.

CHRISTINE M. KORSGAARD is the Arthur Kingsley
Porter Professor of Philosophy at Harvard University. She
is the author of Sources of Normativity (1996), which is an
expanded version of her 1992 Tanner lectures, and of Creating
the Kingdom of Ends (1996). In addition, she has published
numerous articles in moral philosophy.

DEBRA SATZ is associate professor of philosophy and,
by courtesy, political science at Stanford University. She is the
author of a wide range of articles in political philosophy and
is finishing a book, The Limits of the Market, to be published
in 2007.

Preface

DEBRA SATZ

In 2004, distinguished philosopher Harry Frankfurt delivered The Tanner Lectures at Stanford University. The lectures were entitled "Taking Ourselves Seriously" and "Getting it Right." Commentaries were given by Christine Korsgaard (Harvard University); Michael Bratman (Stanford University); Meir Dan-Cohen (University of California-Berkeley, Boalt Hall School of Law); and Eleonore Stump (Saint Louis University). The comments of the first three scholars are included within this volume.

Frankfurt's Tanner Lectures are concerned with the structure of our most basic thinking about how to live. For the last thirty years, since the publication of "Freedom of the Will and the Concept of a Person," Frankfurt has explored in lucid and elegant prose the nature of what it means to be human.

As human beings, we are perhaps uniquely capable of reflecting on ourselves, on who we are and about our reasons for doing what we do. But this cherished ability to reflect, which allows us to be autonomous agents, is also a source of difficulty for us. When we reflect on our desires and goals, we may find that we are ambivalent about them. We may feel uncertain as to whether these are worth caring about at all. The ability to reflect can forge an inner division and lead to self-alienation. Reflection is thus a human achievement, but it is also a source of internal disunity, confusion, and paralysis.

In these lectures, Frankfurt explores the ways that our capacity to love can play a role in restoring unity to our agency. Love gives us ends for our actions, and helps to structure our deliberations. On Frankfurt's view, love is a form of caring especially tied to self-integration. Love plays this role because love is a matter of necessity. We cannot help but care about the things we love—as in Martin Luther's famous remark that here he stands, he can do no other. When we love, we overcome our ambivalence and come to care about people and things wholeheartedly.

Frankfurt denies that either reason or morality can play this role in re-establishing our unified agency. This is because neither reason nor morality can help us to determine what it is we should care about.

The fact that reason tells you that something is valuable to have does not tell you that you should care about having it. A thing may be valuable but not valuable to you. Similarly, the fact that morality commands that we adopt certain ends leaves it an "open question how important it is for us to obey those commands."

On Frankfurt's view, to overcome self-alienation we must find some things with which we can identify whole-heartedly, a set of structured finals ends around which we can organize our lives. These are ends that we cannot but accept, ends whose rejection is literally unthinkable for us. Frankfurt calls these ends "volitional necessities." A person who is subject to a volitional necessity accedes to certain constraints on his will because he is unwilling to oppose it; moreover his unwillingness is itself something that he is unwilling to alter. Very roughly, if caring for something is volitionally necessary for you it is not in your power to give it up at will. It is also not in your power to change this fact about yourself at will, and you wholeheartedly—that is, without any ambivalence on your part—favor all this. Volitional necessities give us powerful reasons to act and a set of values around which to structure our action.

Frankfurt distinguishes between two forms of volitional necessities. First, there are those necessities that all human beings share, simply as human beings. For example, most of the time we are wholeheartedly committed to our continued existence. Second, there are individual volitional necessities—carings that differ from person to person. Frankfurt's suggestion is that the worthiness of what we love—as individuals or as members of a common species—is not important for our ability to figure out how we should live; what matters is that we love something. Volitional necessities are not necessarily grounded in any cognitive process; it can be a brute fact about us that we love someone or something. Our beloved may lack objective qualities of worthiness. In fact, our love may not rest on any reasons at all.

Frankfurt supposes that the necessities to which he alludes involve our wholehearted support. Unlike the addict, who "necessarily" accedes to his addiction because he lacks sufficient strength to defeat it, when I act under a volitional necessity, I am unwilling to alter the constraint this necessity imposes on my actions. I may have the strength of will to alter my love for my son, but I cannot imagine my doing so. Giving up my love right now at will is unthinkable. To the extent that a person is constrained by volitional necessities, there are certain things he cannot but help willing and other things that he cannot bring himself to do. The fact that a person cares about something, or that something is important to her, means that she is disposed to behave in certain ways. Love provides us with "final ends to which we cannot help being bound." It provides us with something to care about. Frankfurt locates the meaning of a person's life in the activity of loving.

The themes of Frankfurt's essays are central for human beings who must cope with the difficulties of being reflective agents while trying to determine how they are to live. This volume presents Frankfurt's latest thinking on this subject along with responses by eminent philosophers and law professors who probe the implications of his work.

In her contribution to this volume, Christine Korsgaard examines the relationship between caring and morality. Does morality give me reasons to act only if I care about morality?

Unlike Frankfurt, Korsgaard thinks that the normativity of morality for an agent does not depend on that agent's directly caring about morality. Morality provides reasons even for the person who thinks morality is unimportant. In her response to Frankfurt, Korsgaard argues that caring has a logic that extends beyond the objects a person cares about. Caring for something, by itself, may commit me to universal shared values, including morality.

Michael Bratman questions whether the volitional necessities of love are indispensable planks in our human psychology. Perhaps other weighty but not necessary carings could ground our self and actions. Some of these weighty reasons may come from a person's desire to maintain a cross-temporal coherence and unity to her life. Indeed, perhaps some of these weighty reasons—projects and plans that are important to her—can override claims of love.

Meir Dan-Cohen explores the implications of Frankfurt's essays for holding people responsible. If I am acting under a volitional necessity, and thus am acting on desires that I wholeheartedly identify with, does that mean I am fully responsible for my actions? If I less than wholeheartedly identify with my desires and actions, am I thereby less responsible? Who determines the degree to which a defendant in a criminal trial identifies with his internal states? The defendant? The jury? Dan-Cohen suggests that we need to think about the drawing of the boundaries of the self as a social and not merely an individual task.

Taken together, this collection of essays and commentaries provide a context for reflecting on the problems of living a reflective life. They are original and highly stimulating essays that should be of interest not only to philosophers, but also to psychologists, law professors, political scientists and, indeed, to anyone who thinks about the meaning and purpose of her life. They are also incredibly enjoyable to read.

The Lectures

Taking Ourselves Seriously

1] I suppose some of you must have noticed that human beings have a tendency to be heavily preoccupied with thinking about themselves. Blind, rollicking spontaneity is not exactly the hallmark of our species. We put considerable effort into trying to get clear about what we are really like, trying to figure out what we are actually up to, and trying to decide whether anything can be done about this. The strong likelihood is that no other animal worries about such matters. Indeed, we humans seem to be the only things around that are even *capable* of taking themselves seriously.

Two features of our nature are centrally implicated in this: our rationality, and our ability to love. Reason and love play critical roles in determining what we think and how we are moved to conduct ourselves. They provide us with decisive motivations, and also with rigorous constraints, in our careers as self-conscious and active creatures. They have a great deal to do, then, with the way we live and with what we are.

We are proud of the human abilities to reason and to love.

This makes us prone to rather egregious ceremonies and excursions of self-congratulation when we imagine that we are actually making use of those abilities. We often pretend that we are exercising one or the other—that we are following reason, or that we are acting out of love—when what is truly going on is something else entirely. In any case, each of the two is emblematic of our humanity, and each is generally acknowledged to merit a special deference and respect. Both are chronically problematic, and the relation between them is obscure.

Taking ourselves seriously means that we are not prepared to accept ourselves just as we come. We want our thoughts, our feelings, our choices, and our behavior to make sense. We are not satisfied to think that our ideas are formed haphazardly, or that our actions are driven by transient and opaque impulses or by mindless decisions. We need to direct ourselves—or at any rate to *believe* that we are directing ourselves—in thoughtful conformity to stable and appropriate norms. We want to get things right.

It is reason and love—the directives of our heads and of our hearts—that we expect to equip us most effectively to accomplish this. Our lives are naturally pervaded, therefore, by an anxious concern to recognize what they demand and to appreciate where they lead. Each has, in its own way, a penetrating and resonant bearing upon our basic condition—the condition of persons, attempting to negotiate the environments of their internal as well as of their external worlds.

Sometimes, to be sure, we energetically resist what reason

or love dictate. Their commands strike us as too burdensome, or as being in some other way unwelcome. So we recoil from them. Perhaps, finally, we reject them altogether. Even then, however, we ordinarily allow that they do possess a genuine and compelling authority. We understand that what they tell us really does count. Indeed, we have no doubt that it counts a great deal—even if, in the end, we prefer not to listen.

Among my aims in these lectures is to explore the roles of reason and of love in our active lives, to consider the relation between them, and to clarify their unmistakable normative authority. In my judgment, as you will see, the authority of practical reason is less fundamental than that of love. In fact, I believe, its authority is grounded in and derives from the authority of love. Now love is constituted by desires, intentions, commitments, and the like. It is essentially—at least as I construe it—a volitional matter. In my view, then, the ultimate source of practical normative authority lies not in reason but in the will.

I hope that you will find my analyses and arguments at least more or less convincing. I also hope, of course, that they will be clear. In this connection, I must confess to being a bit unsettled by a rather mordant piece of advice that comes (I understand) from the quantum physicist Nils Bohr. He is said to have cautioned that one should never speak more clearly than one can think. That must be right; but it is rather daunting. In any event, here goes.

2] What is it about human beings that makes it possible for us to take ourselves seriously? At bottom it is something more primitive, more fundamental to our humanity, and more inconspicuous than either our capacity for reason or our capacity to love. It is our peculiar knack of separating from the immediate content and flow of our own consciousness and introducing a sort of division within our minds. This elementary maneuver establishes an inward-directed, monitoring oversight. It puts in place an elementary reflexive structure, which enables us to focus our attention directly upon ourselves.

When we divide our consciousness in this way, we objectify to ourselves the ingredient items of our ongoing mental life. It is this self-objectification that is particularly distinctive of human mentality. We are unique (probably) in being able simultaneously to be engaged in whatever is going on in our conscious minds, to detach ourselves from it, and to observe it—as it were—from a distance. We are then in a position to form reflexive or higher-order responses to it. For instance, we may approve of what we notice ourselves feeling, or we may disapprove; we may want to remain the sort of person we observe ourselves to be, or we may want to be different. Our division of ourselves situates us to come up with a variety of supervisory desires, intentions, and interventions that pertain to the several constituents and aspects of our conscious life. This has implications of two radically opposed kinds.

On the one hand, it generates a profound threat to our well-being. The inner division that we introduce impairs our capacity for untroubled spontaneity. This is not merely a matter of spoiling our fun. It exposes us to psychological and

spiritual disorders that are nearly impossible to avoid. These
are not only painful; they can be seriously disabling. Facing
ourselves, in the way that internal separation enables us to
do, frequently leaves us chagrined and distressed by what we
see, as well as bewildered and insecure concerning who we
are. Self-objectification facilitates both an inhibiting uncer-
tainty or ambivalence, and a nagging general dissatisfaction
with ourselves. Except in their most extreme forms, these
disorders are too commonplace to be regarded as pathological. They are so integral to our fundamental experience
of ourselves that they serve to define, at least in part, the
inescapable human condition.

By the same token, however, our capacity to divide and
to objectify ourselves provides the foundational structure
for several particularly cherished features of our humanity.
It accounts for the very fact that we possess such a thing
as practical reason; it equips us to enjoy a significant
freedom in the exercise of our will; and it creates for us
the possibility of going beyond simply wanting various
things, and of coming instead to care about them, to regard
them as important to ourselves, and to love them. The
same structural configuration that makes us vulnerable to
disturbing and potentially crippling disabilities also immea-
surably enhances our lives by offering us—as I will try to
explain—opportunities for practical rationality, for freedom
of the will, and for love.

3] When we begin attending to our own feelings and desires,
to our attitudes and motives, and to our dispositions to

behave in certain ways, what we confront is an array of—so to speak—psychic raw material. If we are to amount to more than just biologically qualified members of a certain animal species, we cannot remain passively indifferent to these materials. Developing higher-order attitudes and responses to oneself is fundamental to achieving the status of a responsible person.

To remain wantonly unreflective is the way of nonhuman animals and of small children. They do whatever their impulses move them most insistently to do, without any self-regarding interest in what sort of creature that makes them to be. They are one-dimensional, without the inner depth and complexity that render higher-order responses to oneself possible. Higher-order responses need not be especially thoughtful, or even entirely overt. However, we become responsible persons—quite possibly on the run and without full awareness—only when we disrupt ourselves from an uncritical immersion in our current primary experience, take a look at what is going on in it, and arrive at some resolution concerning what we think about it or how it makes us feel.

Some philosophers have argued that a person becomes responsible for his own character insofar as he shapes it by voluntary choices and actions that cause him to develop habits of discipline or indulgence and hence that make his character what it is. According to Aristotle, no one can help acting as his virtuous or vicious character requires him to act; but in some measure a person's character is nonetheless voluntary, because "we are ourselves . . . part-causes of our state of character" (Nic. Eth., III.5, 1114.b22). In other words, we are responsible for what we are to the extent that we have caused ourselves—by our voluntary behavior—to become that way.

I think Aristotle is wrong about this. Becoming responsible for one's character is not essentially a matter of producing that character but of taking responsibility for it. This happens when a person selectively identifies with certain of his own attitudes and dispositions, whether or not it was he that caused himself to have them. In identifying with them, he incorporates those attitudes and dispositions into himself and makes them his own. What counts is our current effort to define and to manage ourselves, and not the story of how we came to be in the situation with which we are now attempting to cope.

Even if we did cause ourselves to have certain inclinations and tendencies, we can decisively rid ourselves of any responsibility for their continuation by renouncing them and struggling conscientiously to prevent them from affecting our conduct. We will still be responsible, of course, for having brought them about. That cannot be changed. However, we will no longer be responsible for their ongoing presence in our psychic history, or for any conduct to which that may lead. After all, if they do persist, and if they succeed in moving us to act, it will now be only against our will.

4] When we consider the psychic raw materials with which nature and circumstance have provided us, we are sometimes more or less content. They may not exactly please us, or make us proud. Nevertheless, we are willing for them to represent us. We *accept* them as conveying what we really feel, what we truly desire, what we do indeed think, and so on. They do not arouse in us any determined effort to dissociate ourselves from them. Whether with a welcoming approval, or in weary resignation, we *consent* to having them and to being influenced by them.

This willing acceptance of attitudes, thoughts, and feelings transforms their status. They are no longer merely items that happen to appear in a certain psychic history. We have taken responsibility for them as authentic *expressions of ourselves*. We do not regard them as disconnected from us, or as alien intruders by which we are helplessly beset. The fact that we have adopted and sanctioned them makes them intentional and legitimate. Their force is now our force. When they move us, we are therefore not *passive*. We are *active*, because we are being moved just by ourselves.

Being identified with the contents of one's own mind is a very elementary arrangement. It is so ubiquitous, so intimately familiar, and so indispensable to our normal experience, that it is not easy to bring it into sharp focus. It is so natural to us, and as a rule it comes about so effortlessly, that we generally do not notice it at all. In very large measure, it is simply the default condition.

5]   Of course, the default condition does not always prevail. Sometimes we do not participate actively in what goes on in us. It takes place, somehow, but we are just bystanders to it. There are obsessional thoughts, for instance, that disturb us but that we cannot get out of our heads; there are peculiar reckless impulses that make no sense to us, and upon which we would never think of acting; there are hot surges of anarchic emotion that assault us from out of nowhere and that have no recognizable warrant from the circumstances in which they erupt.

These are psychic analogues of the seizures and spasmodic movements that occur at times in our bodies. The fact is that we are susceptible to mental tics, twitches, and convulsions, as well as to physical ones. These are things that *happen to us*. When they occur, we are not participating agents who are expressing what we really think or want or feel. Just as various bodily movements occur without the body being moved by the person whose body it is, so various thoughts, desires, and feelings enter a person's mind without being what that person truly thinks or feels or wants.

Needless to say, however dystonic and disconnected from us these mental events may be, they do occur in our minds—just as the analogous physical events occur nowhere else but in our bodies. They are, at least in a gross, literal sense, our thoughts, our feelings, and our desires. Moreover, they often provide important indications of what else is going on in our minds. Uncontrollably spasmodic movements of the limbs are likely to be symptomatic of some deeper and otherwise hidden physical condition. Similarly, the fact that I have an obsessional thought that the sun is about to explode, or a wild impulse to jump out the window, may reveal something very significant about what is going on in my unconscious. Still, that is not what I really think about the sun; nor does the impulse to jump express something that I really want to do.

6] What a person finds in himself may not just seem oddly
disconnected from him. It may be dangerously antithetical
to his intentions and to his conception of himself. Some
of the psychic raw material that we confront may be so
objectionable to us that we cannot permit it to determine our
attitudes or our behavior. We cannot help having that dark
side. However, we are resolved to keep it from producing any
direct effect upon the design and conduct of our lives.

These unacceptable intruders arouse within us, then, an
anxious disposition to resist. By a kind of psychic immune
response—which may be mobilized without our even being
aware of it—we push them away, and we introduce barriers of
repression and inhibition between them and ourselves. That
is, we dissociate ourselves from them, and seek to prevent
them from being at all effective. Instead of incorporating
them, we *externalize* them.

This means that we deny them any entitlement to supply
us with motives or with reasons. They are outlawed and
disenfranchised. We refuse to recognize them as grounds
for deciding what to think or what to do. Regardless of
how insistent they may be, we assign their claims no place
whatever in the order of preferences and priorities that we
establish for our deliberate choices and acts. The fact that
we continue to be powerfully moved by them gives them no
rational claim. Even if an externalized desire turns out to be
irresistible, its dominion is merely that of a tyrant. It has, for
us, no legitimate authority.

Some philosophers maintain that, just in virtue of having
a desire, a person *necessarily* has a reason for trying to satisfy

it. The reason may not be a very strong one; there may be much better reasons to perform another action instead. Nevertheless, it counts for something. The very fact that a person wants to do something always means, on this view, that there is at least that much of a reason in favor of his doing it.

However, the mere fact that a person has a desire does not give him a reason. What it gives him is a problem. He has the problem of whether to identify with the desire and thus validate it as eligible for satisfaction, or whether to dissociate himself from it, treat it as categorically unacceptable, and try to suppress it or rid himself of it entirely. If he identifies with the desire, he acknowledges that satisfying it is to be assigned *some* position—however inferior—in the order of his preferences and priorities. If he externalizes the desire, he determines to give it no position in that order at all.

7] Reflexivity and identification have fundamental roles in the constitution of practical reason. Indeed, it is only by virtue of these elementary maneuvers that we *have* such a thing as practical reason. Without their intervention, we could not regard any fact as giving us a reason for performing any action.

When does a fact give us a reason for performing an action? It does so when it suggests that performing the action would help us reach one or another of our goals. For example, the fact that it is raining gives me a reason for carrying an umbrella insofar as doing that would be helpful as a means to my goal of keeping dry.

Having a goal is not the same, however, as simply being

moved by a desire. Suppose I have a desire to kill someone, and that firing my pistol at him would be an effective way to accomplish this. Does that mean I have a reason to fire my pistol at him? In fact, I have a reason for doing that only if killing the man is not just an outcome for which a desire happens to be occurring in me. The desire must be one that I accept and with which I identify. The outcome must be one that I really want.

Suppose that the man in question is my beloved son, that our relationship has always been a source of joy for me, and that my desire to kill him has no evident connection to any-thing that has been going on. The desire is wildly exogenous; it comes entirely out of the blue. No doubt it signifies God knows what unconscious fantasy, which is ordinarily safely repressed. In any case, it instantly arouses in me a massive and wholehearted revulsion. I do whatever I can to distance myself from it, and to block any likelihood that it will lead me to act.

The murderous inclination is certainly real. I do have that lethal desire. However, it is not true that I want to kill my son. I don't really want to kill him. Therefore, I don't have any reason to fire my pistol at him. It would be preposterous to insist that I do have at least a weak reason to shoot him—a reason upon which I refrain from acting only because it is overridden by much stronger reasons for wanting him to remain alive. The fact that shooting him is likely to kill him gives me *no reason at all* to shoot him, even though it is true that I have a desire to kill him and that shooting him might do the trick. Because the desire is one with which I do not identify, my having it does not mean that killing my son is actually among my goals.

8] Practical reasoning is, in part, a procedure through which we determine what we have most reason to do in order to reach our goals. There could be no deliberative exercise of practical reason if we were related to our desires only in the one-dimensional way that animals of nonreflective species are related to whatever inner experience they have. Like them, we would be mutely immersed in whatever impulses happen at the moment to be moving us; and we would act upon whichever of those impulses happened to be most intense. We would be no more able than they are to decide what we have reason to do because, like them, we would be unable to construe anything as being for us an end or a goal.

In fact, without reflexivity we could not make decisions at all. To make a decision is to make up one's mind. This is an inherently reflexive act, which the mind performs upon itself. Subhuman animals cannot perform it because they cannot divide their consciousness. Because they cannot take themselves apart, they cannot put their minds back together. If we lacked our distinctive reflexive and volitional capacities, making decisions would be impossible for us too.

That would not alter the fact that, like all animals in some degree, we would be capable of behaving intelligently. Being intelligent and being rational are not the same. When I attempt to swat an insect, the insect generally flies or scurries rapidly away to a place that is more difficult for me to reach. This behavior reduces the likelihood that it will die. The insect's self-preservative movements are not structured in detail by instinct. They are not inflexibly modular or tropistic. They are continuously adjusted to be effective in the particular, and often rapidly changing, circumstances at hand. In other words, the insect—although it does not deliberate or reason—behaves intelligently. Even if we too were unable to reason or to deliberate, we too would nevertheless often still be able—by appropriately adaptive adjustments in our behavior—to find our way intelligently to the satisfaction of our desires.

9] Let us suppose that a certain motive has been rejected as unacceptable. Our attempt to immunize ourselves against it may not work. The resistance we mobilize may be insufficient. The externalized impulse or desire may succeed, by its sheer power, in defeating us and forcing its way. In that case, the outlaw imposes itself upon us without authority, and against our will. This suggests a useful way of understanding what it is for a person's will to be free.

When we are doing exactly what we want to do, we are acting freely. A free act is one that a person performs simply because he wants to perform it. Enjoying freedom of action consists in maintaining this harmonious accord between what we do and what we want to do.

Now sometimes, similarly, the desire that motivates a person as he acts is precisely the desire by which he wants to be motivated. For instance, he wants to act from feelings of warmth and generosity; and in fact he is warm and generous in what he does. There is a straightforward parallel here between a free action and a free will. Just as we act freely when what we do is what we want to do, so we will freely when what we want is what we want to want—that is, when the will behind what we do is exactly the will by which we want our action to be moved. A person's will is free, on this account, when there is in him a certain volitional unanimity. The desire that governs him as he is acting is in agreement with a higher-order volition concerning what he wants to be his governing desire.

Of course, there are bound to be occasions when the desire that motivates us when we act is a desire by which we do not want to be motivated. Instead of being moved by the warm and generous feelings that he would prefer to express, a person's conduct may be driven by a harsh envy, of which he disapproves but that he has been unable to prevent from gaining control. On occasions like that, the will is not free.

But suppose that we are doing what we want to do, that our motivating first-order desire to perform the action is exactly the desire by which we want our action to be motivated, and that there is no conflict in us between this motive and any desire at any higher order. In other words, suppose we are thoroughly wholehearted both in what we are doing and in what we want. Then there is no respect in which we are being violated or defeated or coerced. Neither our desires nor the conduct to which they lead are imposed upon us without our consent or against our will. We are acting just as we want, and our motives are just what we want them to be. Then so far as I can see, we have on that occasion all the freedom for which finite creatures can reasonably hope. Indeed, I believe that we have as much freedom as it is possible for us even to conceive.

10]   Notice that this has nothing to do with whether our actions, our desires, or our choices are causally determined. The widespread conviction among thoughtful people that there is a radical opposition between free will and determinism is, on this account, a red herring. The possibility that everything is necessitated by antecedent causes does not threaten our freedom. What it threatens is our power. Insofar as we are governed by causal forces, we are not omnipotent. That has no bearing, however, upon whether we can be free.

As finite creatures, we are unavoidably subject to forces other than our own. What we do is, at least in part, the outcome of causes that stretch back indefinitely into the past. This means that we cannot design our lives from scratch, entirely unconstrained by any antecedent and external conditions. However, there is no reason why a sequence of causes, outside our control and indifferent to our interests and wishes, might not happen to lead to the harmonious volitional structure in which the free will of a person consists. That same structural unanimity might also conceivably be an outcome of equally blind chance. Whether causal determinism is true or whether it is false, then, the wills of at least some of us may at least sometimes be free. In fact, this freedom is clearly not at all uncommon.

11]   In the Scholium to Proposition 52 in part 4 of his *Ethics*, Spinoza declares that "the highest good we can hope for" is what he refers to as "acquiescentia in se ipso." Various translators render this Latin phrase into English as "self-contentment," "self-esteem," or "satisfaction with oneself." These translations are a little misleading. The good to which Spinoza refers is certainly not to be confused with the contentment or pride or satisfaction that people sometimes award themselves because of what they think they have accomplished, or because of the talents or other personal gifts with which they believe they are endowed. It is not Spinoza's view that the highest good for which we can hope has to do either with successful achievement or with vanity or pride.

There is something to be said for a bluntly literal construction of his Latin. That would have Spinoza mean that the highest good consists in *acquiescence to oneself*—that is, in acquiescence to being the person that one is, perhaps not enthusiastically but nonetheless with a willing acceptance of the motives and dispositions by which one is moved in what one does. This would amount to an inner harmony that comes to much the same thing as having a free will. It would bring with it the natural satisfaction—or the contentment or self-esteem—of being just the kind of person one wants to be.

Unquestionably, it is a very good thing to be in this sense contented with oneself. Spinoza does not say that it is the best thing one can hope for; he doesn't say even that it is enough to make life good. After all, it may be accompanied by terrible suffering, disappointment, and failure. So why say, as he does, that it is the highest thing for which one can hope?

Perhaps because it resolves the deepest problem. In our transition beyond naive animality, we separate from ourselves and disrupt our original unreflective spontaneity. This puts us at risk to varieties of inner fragmentation, dissonance, and disorder. Accepting ourselves reestablishes the wholeness that was undermined by our elementary constitutive maneuvers of division and distancing. When we are acquiescent to ourselves, or willing freely, there is no conflict within the structure of our motivations and desires. We have successfully negotiated our distinctively human complexity. The unity of our self has been restored.

12] The volitional unity in which freedom of the will consists is purely structural. The fact that a person's desire is freely willed implies nothing as to what is desired or as to whether the person actually cares in the least about it. In an idle moment, we may have an idle inclination to flick away a crumb; and we may be quite willing to be moved by that desire. Nonetheless, we recognize that flicking the crumb would be an altogether inconsequential act. We want to perform it, but performing it is of no importance to us. We really don't care about it at all.

What this means is not that we assign it a very low priority. To regard it as truly of no importance to us is to be willing to give up having any interest in it whatever. We have no desire, in other words, to continue wanting to flick away the crumb. It would be all the same to us if we completely ceased wanting to do that. When we do care about something, we go beyond wanting it. We want to go on wanting it, at least until the goal has been reached. Thus, we feel it as a lapse on our part if we neglect the desire, and we are disposed to take steps to refresh the desire if it should tend to fade. The caring entails, in other words, a commitment to the desire

Willing freely means that the self is at that time harmoniously integrated. There is, within it, a synchronic coherence. Caring about something implies a diachronic coherence, which integrates the self across time. Like free will, then, caring has an important structural bearing upon the character of our lives. By our caring, we maintain various thematic continuities in our volitions. We engage ourselves in guiding the course of our desires. If we cared about nothing, we would play no active role in designing the successive configurations of our will.

The fact that there are things that we do care about is plainly more basic to us—more constitutive of our essential nature—than what those things are. Nevertheless, *what* we care about—that is, what we consider important to ourselves—is obviously critical to the particular course and to the particular quality of our lives. This naturally leads people who take themselves seriously to wonder how to get it right. It leads them to confront fundamental issues of normativity. How are we to determine what, if anything, we should care about? What makes something genuinely important to us?

13] Some things are important to us only because we care about them. Who wins the American League batting title this year is important to me if I am the kind of baseball fan who cares about that sort of thing, but probably not otherwise. My close friends are especially important to me; but if I did not actually care about those individuals, they would be no more important to me than anyone else.

Of course, many things are important to people even though they do not actually care about them. Vitamins were important to the ancient Greeks, who could not have cared about them because they had no idea that there were such things. Vitamins are, however, indispensable to health; and the Greeks did care about that. What people do not care about may nonetheless be quite important to them, obviously, because of its value as a means to something that they do in fact care about.

In my view, it is only in virtue of what we actually care about that anything is important to us.[1] The world is everywhere infused for us with importance; many things are important to us. That is because there are many things that we care about just for themselves, and many that stand in pertinent instrumental relationships to those things. If there were nothing that we cared about—if our response to the world were utterly and uniformly flat—there would be no reason for us to care about anything.

14]   Does this mean that it is all simply up to us—that what is truly important to us depends just upon what goes on in our minds? Surely there are certain things that are *inherently* and *objectively* important and worth caring about, and other things that are not. Regardless of what our own desires or attitudes or other mental states may happen to be, surely there are some things that we should care about, and others that we certainly should not care about. Is it not unmistakably apparent that people should at least care about adhering to the requirements of morality, by which all of us are inescapably bound no matter what our individual inclinations or preferences may be?

Some philosophers believe that the authority of morality is as austerely independent of personal contingencies as is the authority of logic. Indeed, their view is that moral principles are grounded in the same fundamental rationality as logically necessary truths. For instance, one advocate of this moral rationalism says: "Just as there are rational requirements on thought, there are rational requirements on action"; and because "the requirements of ethics are rational requirements . . . , the motive for submitting to them must be one which it would be contrary to reason to ignore."[2] On this account, failure to submit to the moral law is irrational. The authority of the moral law is the authority of reason itself.

The normative authority of reason, however, cannot be what accounts for the normative authority of morality. There must be some other explanation of why we should be moral. For one thing, our response to immoral conduct is very different from our response to errors in reasoning. Contradicting oneself or reasoning fallaciously is not, as such, a moral lapse. People who behave immorally incur a distinctive kind of opprobrium, which is quite unlike the normal attitude toward those who reason poorly. Our response to sinners is not the same as our response to fools.

Moreover, if it were possible for people to justify their conduct strictly by reason—that is, with rigorous proofs

demonstrating that acting otherwise would be irrational—
that would provide no advantage to morality. In fact, it would
render the claims of morality far less compelling, because it
would take people off the hook. After all, being convinced by
proofs does not implicate any of a person's individual preferences or predilections. Reason *necessitates* assent, and leaves
no room for individual choice. It is entirely impersonal. It
does not reveal character.

Construing the basis of morality rationalistically misses
the whole point of moral norms. Morality is essentially
designed to put people on the hook. Whether or not a person
adheres to the moral law is not supposed to be independent
of the kind of person he is. It is presumed to reveal something about him deeper and more intimate than his cognitive
acuity. Moral principles cannot rest, therefore, simply upon
rational requirements. There must be something behind the
authority of the moral law besides reason.

15]   Let us assume, then, that moral authority cannot be
satisfactorily established by invoking just the bloodless
support of strict rationality. Is there not a sufficient basis of
some other kind for recognizing that moral requirements
(and perhaps normative requirements of various other types
as well) are genuinely important in themselves, regardless of
anyone's beliefs or feelings or inclinations? In my judgment,
there is not. There can be no rationally warranted criteria for
establishing anything as inherently important.

Here is one way to see why. Nothing is important if
everything would be exactly the same with it as without it.

Things are important only if they make a difference. However, the fact that they do make a difference is not enough to show that they are important. Some differences are too trivial. A thing is important only if it makes an important difference. Thus, we cannot know whether something is important until we already know how to tell whether the difference it makes is important.

The unlimited regress to which this leads is clearly unacceptable. If it were possible for attributions of inherent importance to be rationally grounded, they would have to be grounded in something besides other attributions of inherent importance. The truth is, I believe, that it is possible to ground judgments of importance only in judgments concerning what people care about. Nothing is truly important to a person unless it makes a difference that he actually cares about. Importance is never inherent. It is always dependent upon the attitudes and dispositions of the individual. Unless a person knows what he *already* cares about, therefore, he cannot determine what he has reason to care about.

The most fundamental question for anyone to raise concerning importance cannot be the normative question of what he *should* care about. That question can be answered only on the basis of a prior answer to a question that is not normative at all, but straightforwardly factual—namely, the question of what he actually does care about.[3] If he attempts to suspend all of his convictions, and to adopt a stance that is conscientiously neutral and uncommitted, he cannot even begin to inquire methodically into what it would be reasonable for him to care about. No one can pull himself up by his own bootstraps.

16] What we care about has to do with our particular interests and inclinations. If what we *should* care about depends upon what we *do* care about, any answer to the normative question must be derived from considerations that are manifestly subjective. This may make it appear that what we should care about is indeed up to us, and that it is therefore likely to vary from one person to another and to be unstable over time.

Answers to the normative question are certainly up to us in the sense that they depend upon what we care about. However, what we care about is not always up to us. Our will is not invariably subject to our will. We cannot have, simply for the asking, whatever will we want. There are some things that we cannot help caring about. Our caring about them consists of desires and dispositions that are not under our immediate voluntary control. We are committed in ways that we cannot directly affect. Our volitional character does not change just because we wish it to change, or because we resolve that it do so. Insofar as answers to the normative question depend upon carings that we cannot alter at will, what we should care about is not up to us at all.

Among the things that we cannot help caring about are the things that we love. Love is not a voluntary matter. It may at times be possible to contrive arrangements that make love more likely or that make it less likely. Still, we cannot bring ourselves to love, or to stop loving, by an act of will alone—that is, merely by choosing to do so. And sometimes we cannot affect it by any means whatsoever.

The actual causes of love are various and often difficult to trace. It is sometimes maintained that genuine love can be aroused only by the perceived value of the beloved object. The value of the beloved is what captivates the lover, and moves him to love. If he were not responsive to its value, he would not love it. I do not deny that love may be aroused in this way. However, love does not require a response by the lover to any real or imagined value in what he loves. Parents do not ordinarily love their children so much, for example, because they perceive that their children possess exceptional value. In fact, it is the other way around: the children seem to the parents to be valuable, and they are valuable to the parents, only because the parents love them. Parents have been known to love—quite genuinely—children that they themselves recognize as lacking any particular inherent merit.

As I understand the nature of love, the lover does not depend for his loving upon reasons of any kind. Love is not a conclusion. It is not an outcome of reasoning, or a consequence of reasons. It *creates* reasons. What it means to love is, in part, to take the fact that a certain action would serve the good of the beloved as an especially compelling reason for performing that action.

17]   We care about many things only for their instrumental value. They are intermediate goals for us, which we pursue as means to other things. Conceivably, a person's goals might all be intermediate: whatever he wants, he wants just for the sake of another thing; and he wants that other thing just in order to obtain something else; and so on. That sort of life could certainly keep a person busy. However, running endlessly from one thing to another, with no conclusive destinations, could not provide any full satisfaction because it would provide no sense of genuine achievement. We need final ends, whose value is not merely instrumental. I believe that our final ends are provided and legitimated by love.

Love is paradigmatically personal. What people love differs, and may conflict. There is often, unfortunately, no way to adjudicate such conflicts. The account of normativity that I have been giving may therefore seem excessively skeptical. Many people are convinced that our final ends and values—most urgently our moral values—must be impregnably secured by reason and must possess an inescapable authority that is altogether independent of anyone's personal desires and attitudes. What we should care about, they insist, must be determined by a reality entirely other than ourselves. My account is likely to strike them as radically neglectful of these requirements. They will have the idea that it is unacceptably noncognitive and relativistic. I think that idea is wrong, and I will try to correct it in my next lecture.

Getting It Right

1] Suppose you are trying to figure out how to live. You want to know what goals to pursue and what limits to respect. You need to get clear about what counts as a good reason in deliberations concerning choice and action. It is important to you to understand what is important to you.

In that case, your most fundamental problem is not to understand how to identify what is valuable. Nor is it to discover what the principles of morality demand, forbid, and permit. You are concerned with how to make specific concrete decisions about what to aim at and how to behave. Neither judgments of value in general nor moral judgments in particular can settle this for you.

From the fact that we consider something to be valuable, it does not follow that we need to be concerned with it. There are many objects, activities, and states of affairs that we acknowledge to be valuable but in which we quite reasonably take no interest because they do not fit into our lives. Other things, perhaps even of lesser value, are more important to us. What we are actually to care about—what we are to regard as really important to us—cannot be based simply upon judgments concerning what has the most value.

In a similar way, morality too fails to get down to the bottom of things. The basic concern of morality is with how to conduct ourselves in our relations with other people. Now why should *that* be, always and in all circumstances, the most important thing in our lives? No doubt it is important; but, so far as I am aware, there is no convincing argument that it must invariably override everything else. Even if it were entirely clear what the moral law commands, it would remain an open question how important it is for us to obey those commands. We would still have to decide how much to care about morality. Morality itself cannot satisfy us about that.

What a person really needs to know, in order to know how to live, is what to care about and how to measure the relative importance to him of the various things about which he cares. These are the deepest, as well as the most immediate, normative concerns of our active lives. To the extent that we succeed in resolving them, we are able to identify and to order our goals. We possess an organized repertoire of final ends. That puts us in a position to determine, both in general and in particular instances, what we have reason to do. It is our understanding of what to care about, then, that is the ultimate touchstone and basis of our practical reasoning.

2]   So, what *are* we to care about? This is not a matter that we can settle arbitrarily, or by deploying some shallow and unstable measure. In designing and committing our lives, we cannot rely upon casual impulse. Our deliberations and our actions must be guided by procedures and standards in which it is appropriate for us to have a mature confidence. The final ends by which we govern ourselves require authentication by some decisive rational warrant.

There is a famous passage in David Hume's *Treatise of Human Nature* that appears to rule out the possibility of providing any rational basis for deciding what we are to care about. Even the most grotesque preferences, Hume insists, are not irrational. He declares, for instance, that "'tis not contrary to reason to prefer the destruction of the whole world to the scratching of my finger."[1]

Now it is true that this preference involves no purely logical mistake. So far as logic alone is concerned, it is unobjectionable. Someone who chooses to protect his finger from a trivial injury at the cost of unlimited destruction elsewhere is not thereby guilty of any contradiction or faulty inference. In this purely formal sense of rationality, his choice is not at all irrational.

But what would we say of someone who made that choice? We would say he must be *crazy*. In other words, despite the unassailability of his preference on logical grounds, we would consider both it and him to be wildly irrational. Caring more about a scratched finger than about "destruction of the whole world" is not just an unappealing personal quirk. It is lunatic. Anybody who has that preference is inhuman.

3] When we characterize the person in Hume's example as "crazy," or as "lunatic," or as "inhuman," these epithets do not function as mere vituperative rhetoric. They are literal denials that the person is a rational creature. There is a familiar mode of rationality, then, that is not exclusively defined by a priori, formal necessities. Hume's madman may be as competent as we are in designing valid chains of inference and in distinguishing between what is and what is not logically possible. His irrationality is not fundamentally a cognitive deficiency at all. He is volitionally irrational. He has a defect of the will, which bears upon how he is disposed to choose and to act.

Our basis for considering him to be volitionally irrational is not that his preferences happen to be merely very different from ours. It is that the relative importance to him of protecting his finger and of destroying the world is altogether incommensurate with how much we care about those things. He is moved to bring about unimaginable destruction for a reason that strikes us as so inconsequential as hardly to justify incurring any cost at all. An outcome from which we recoil in horror is, to him, positively attractive. The critical point has to do with possibilities: he is prepared to implement voluntarily a choice that we could not, under any circumstances, bring ourselves to make.

4] There are structural analogues between the requirements of volitional rationality and the strictly formal, a priori requirements of pure reason. Both modes of rationality limit what is possible, and each imposes a corresponding necessity. The boundaries of formal rationality are defined by the necessary truths of logic, to which no alternatives are conceivable. The boundaries of volitional rationality are defined by contingencies that effectively constrain the will. They limit what it is in fact possible for us to care about, what we can accept as reasons for action, and what we can actually bring ourselves to do. Violations of volitional rationality are not *inconceivable*. Rather, what stands in their way is that they are *unthinkable*.

Being volitionally rational is not just a matter of the choices that a person actually makes. It involves being incapable, under any circumstances, of making certain choices. If someone attempts to reach a cool and balanced judgment about whether it would be a good idea to destroy the entire world in order to avoid being scratched on his finger, that is not a demonstration of sturdy rationality. Even if he finally concludes that destroying the world to protect his finger is after all not such a good idea, the fact that he had to deliberate about this would make it clear that something is wrong with him.

Rationality does not permit us to be open-minded and judicious about everything. It requires that certain choices be utterly out of the question. Just as a person transgresses the boundaries of formal reason if he supposes of some self-contradictory state of affairs that it might really be possible, so he transgresses the boundaries of volitional rationality if he regards certain choices as genuine options.

A rational person cannot bring himself to do various things that, so far as his power and skill are concerned, he would otherwise be entirely capable of doing. He may think that a certain action is appropriate, or even mandated; but when the chips are down, he finds that he just cannot go through with it. He cannot mobilize his will to implement his judgment. No reasons are good enough to move him actually to carry out the action. He cannot bring himself to destroy the world in order to avoid a scratch on his finger. In virtue of the necessities by which his will is constrained, making that choice is not among his genuine options. It is simply unthinkable.

5]   What makes it unthinkable? Why are we unable to bring ourselves to do certain things? What accounts for our inability, or our inflexible refusal, to include among our alternatives various actions that we are otherwise quite capable of performing? What is the ground of the constraints upon our will that volitional rationality entails?

One view is that these volitional necessities are responses to an independent normative reality. On this account, certain things are inherently important. They therefore provide incontrovertible reasons for acting in certain ways. This is not a function of our attitudes or beliefs or desires, or of subjective factors of any kind. It does not depend in any way upon the condition of our will, or upon what we happen to regard as reasons for acting. In virtue of their unequivocal objectivity, moreover, these reasons possess an inescapable normative authority. It is the natural authority of the real, to which all rational thought and conduct must seek to conform.

In some way—just how is commonly left rather obscure— the independent reality of these reasons becomes apparent to us. We recognize, with a vivid clarity, that various things are inherently important. Then we cannot help accepting the authority of the reasons that they provide. It is impossible for us to deny, or to hold back from acknowledging, the importance that is—so to speak—right before our eyes. Seeing is believing. Thus, our will comes to be constrained by the forceful immediacy of reality.

This is the doctrine of "normative realism." It holds that there are objective reasons for us to act in various ways, whether we know them, or care about them, or not. If we fail to appreciate and to accept those reasons, we are making a mistake. Some philosophers presume that normative realism is implicitly supported by the presumption that, as Robert Adams puts it, "keeping an eye out for possible corrections of our views is an important part of the seriousness of normative discourse."[2] In their view, our concern to avoid mistakes— our belief that we need to get our normative judgments and attitudes right—"strongly favors" the supposition that the importance of reasons is inherent in them and that practical reason is therefore securely grounded in the independent reality of its governing norms.

6]   My own view is different. I do not believe that anything is inherently important. In my judgment, normativity is not a feature of a reality that is independent of us. The standards of volitional rationality and of practical reason are grounded, so far as I can see, only in ourselves. More particularly, they are grounded only in what we cannot help caring about and cannot help considering important.

Our judgments concerning normative requirements

can certainly get things wrong. There is indeed an objective normative reality, which is not up to us and to which we are bound to conform. However, this reality is not objective in the sense of being entirely outside of our minds. Its objectivity consists just in the fact that it is outside the scope of our voluntary control.

Normative truths require that we submit to them. What makes them inescapable, however, is not that they are grounded in an external and independent reality. They are inescapable because they are determined by volitional necessities that we cannot alter or elude. In matters concerning practical normativity, the demanding objective reality that requires us to keep an eye out for possible correction of our views is a reality that is within ourselves.

7]   Let me begin to illustrate and to explain this by considering what I suppose everyone will agree is a clear paradigm of something that is genuinely important to us.

Except perhaps under extraordinary conditions, the fact that an action would protect a person's life is universally acknowledged to be a reason for that person to perform the action. He may have a better reason for doing something else instead. There may even be entirely convincing reasons for him to prefer to die. However, self-defense is rarely (if ever) either thought to be a wholly irrelevant consideration in the evaluation of alternatives, or thought to be in itself a reason against performing an action. Generally it is acknowledged without reserve to be at least a reason in favor of performing any action that contributes to it.

As a source of reasons for acting, our interest in staying alive has enormous scope and resonance. There is no area of human activity in which it does not generate reasons—sometimes weaker, sometimes stronger—for doing certain things or for doing things in a certain way. Self-preservation is perhaps the most commanding, the most protean, and the least questioned of our final ends. Its importance is recognized by everyone, and it radiates everywhere. It infuses importance into innumerable objects and activities, and it helps to justify innumerable decisions. Practical reason could hardly get along without it.

8]   How come? What accounts for the fact that we are always at least minimally attentive to the task of protecting our lives? What is it about survival that makes it at all important to us? What warrants our invariable acceptance of self-preservation as a reason that supports preferring one course of action over another?

Many people claim to believe that every human life is intrinsically valuable, regardless of how it is lived. Some individuals profess that what they are doing with their lives, or what they are likely to do with them, gives their lives a special importance. However, even when people have ideas like these about the value or importance of human life, that is ordinarily not the sole or even the primary explanation of why they are determined to go on living. It is not what really accounts for the fact that, in making decisions concerning what to do, they regard preserving their lives as a significant, justifying consideration. Someone who acts in self-defense is universally conceded to have a pertinent reason for doing what he does, regardless of how he or others may evaluate his life.

Another view purports to identify reasons for living that do not require any assumption concerning the value of our lives. One of the best recent moral philosophers, the late Bernard Williams, suggests that it is a person's ambitions and plans—what he calls the person's "projects"—that provide "the motive force [that] propels [the person] into the future, and gives him a reason for living." These projects are "a condition of his having any interest in being around" in the world at all. Unless we have projects that we care about, Williams insists, "it is unclear why [we] should go on."[3] In other words, we have a reason to do what it takes to go on living if we have projects that require our survival, but not otherwise.

That can't be right. It seems to me that what Williams says pertains just to people who are seriously depressed. The individuals he describes have no natural vitality. Their lives are inert, lacking any inherent momentum or flow. The movement from one moment to the next does not come to these people in the usual way—as a matter of course. They need a special push. They will move willingly into the future only if they are "propelled" into doing so. Unless they can supply themselves with an effectively propulsive fuel—"projects"—they will conclude that there is no reason for them to go on at all, and they will lose interest in being around.

Surely Williams has it backward. Our interest in living does not commonly depend upon our having projects that we desire to pursue. It's the other way around: we are interested in having worthwhile projects because we do intend to go on living, and we would prefer not to be bored. When we learn that a person has acted to defend his own life, we do not need to inquire whether he had any projects in order to recognize that he had a reason for doing whatever it was that he did.

9]   What ordinarily moves us to go on living, and also to accept our desire to continue living as a legitimate reason for acting, is not that we think we have reasons of any kind for wanting to survive. Our desire to live, and our readiness to invoke this desire as generating reasons for performing actions that contribute to that end, are not themselves based on reasons. They are based on love. They derive from and express the fact that, presumably as an outcome of natural selection, we love life. That is, we love living.

This does not mean that we especially enjoy it. Frequently we do not. Many people willingly put up with a great deal of suffering simply in order to stay alive. It is true, of course, that some people are so very miserable that they do really want to die. But this hardly shows that they do not love life. It only shows that they hate misery. What they would certainly prefer, if only they could arrange it, is not to end their lives but just to end the misery.

The desire to go on living is not only universal. It is irreducible. It is only if our prerational urge to preserve our lives has somehow become drastically attentuated that we demand reasons for preserving them. Otherwise, we do not require reasons at all. Our interest in self-preservation is a lavishly fecund source of reasons for choice and for action. However, it is not itself grounded in reasons. It is grounded in love.

10]   In addition to their interest in staying alive, people generally have various other similarly primitive and protean concerns as well, which also provide them with reasons for acting. For instance, we cannot help caring about avoiding crippling injury and illness, about maintaining at least some minimal contact with other human beings, and about being free from chronic suffering and endlessly stupefying boredom. We love being intact and healthy, being satisfied, and being in touch. We cannot bring ourselves to be wholly indifferent to these things, much less categorically opposed to them. To a considerable degree, moreover, it is our concerns for them that give rise to the more detailed interests and ambitions that we develop in response to the specific content and course of our experience.

These fundamental necessities of the will are not transient creatures of social prescription or of cultural habit. Nor are they constituted by peculiarities of individual taste or judgment. They are solidly entrenched in our human nature from the start. Indeed, they are elementary constituents of volitional reason itself. It is conceivable, of course, that someone might actually not care a bit about these presumptively universal final ends. There is no logical barrier to rejecting them altogether or to being devoted to their opposites. Loving death, or incapacity, or isolation, or continuously vacant or distressing experience involves no contradiction. If a person did love those things, however, we would be unable to make sense of his life.

It is not terribly difficult to understand that a sensible person might regard certain states of affairs as giving him sufficient reason to commit suicide, or to incur crippling injuries, or to seek radical and permanent isolation, or to accept endless boredom or misery. What would be unintelligible is someone pursuing those things for their own sakes, rather than just to attain other goals that he cared about more. We could not empathize with, or expect ourselves to be understood by, someone who loves death or disability or unhappiness. We would be unable to grasp how he could possibly be drawn to what we cannot help being so naturally driven to avoid. His preferences, his deliberations, and his actions are guided by final ends that to us would be flatly incomprehensible. It makes no sense to us that anyone could love them.

11]   What is at stake here is not a matter of avoiding mistakes and getting things right. The volitionally irrational lover of death or disability or suffering has not overlooked something, or misunderstood something, or miscalculated, or committed any sort of error. From our point of view, his will is not so much in error as it is deformed. His attitudes do not depend upon beliefs that might be demonstrated by cogent evidence or argument to be false. It is impossible to reason with him meaningfully concerning his ends, any more than we could reason with someone who refuses to accept any proposition unless it is self-contradictory.

Many philosophers believe that an act is right only if it can be justified to other rational beings. For this to be plausible, it is not enough that the rationality of the others be merely of the formal variety. Those whom we seek to convince must be volitionally rational as well. If they are not, then their practical reasoning—however formally correct it may be—builds upon a foundation that is in radical opposition to ours. What justifies something to us will, to them, serve only to condemn it. We can therefore do no more with them than to express the bewilderment and revulsion that are inspired in us by the grotesque ends and ideals that they love.

12]   So what is love? My conception does not aim at encompassing every feature of the hopelessly inchoate set of conditions that people think of as instances of love. The phenomenon that I have in mind includes only what is, for my purposes, philosophically indispensable. Most especially, it is not to be confused with romantic love, infatuation, dependency, obsession, lust, or similar varieties of psychic turbulence.

As I construe it, love is a particular mode of caring. It is an involuntary, nonutilitarian, rigidly focused, and—as is any mode of caring—self-affirming concern for the existence and the good of what is loved. The object of love can be almost anything—a life, a quality of experience, a person, a group, a moral ideal, a nonmoral ideal, a tradition, whatever. The lover's concern is rigidly focused in that there can be no equivalent substitute for its object, which he loves in its sheer particularity and not as an exemplar of some general type. His concern is nonutilitarian in that he cares about his beloved for its own sake, rather than only as a means to some other goal.

It is in the nature of the lover's concern that he is invested in his beloved. That is, he benefits when his beloved flourishes; and he suffers when it is harmed. Another way of putting it is that the lover identifies himself with what he loves. This consists in the lover accepting the interests of his beloved as his own. Love does not necessarily include a desire for union of any other kind. It does not entail any interest in reciprocity or symmetry in the relationship between lover and beloved. Moreover, because the beloved may be entirely unaware of the love, and may be entirely unaffected by it, loving entails no special obligation to the beloved.

Loving is risky. Linking oneself to the interests of another, and exposing oneself to their vicissitudes, warrants a certain prudence. We can sometimes take steps that inhibit us from loving, or steps that stimulate us to love; more or less effective precautions and therapies may be available, by means of which a person can influence whether love develops or whether it lasts. Love is nonetheless involuntary, in that it is not under the immediate control of the will. We cannot love—or stop loving—merely by deciding to do so.

The causes of love are multifarious and frequently obscure. In any event, love is not essentially a matter of judgment or of reasoned choice. People often think of what causes them to love something as giving them reasons to love it. However, loving is not the rationally determined outcome of even an implicit deliberative or evaluative process. Parmenides said that love is "the first-born offspring of necessity."4 We come to love because we cannot help loving. Love requires no reasons, and it can have anything as its cause.

On the other hand, love is a powerful source of reasons. When a lover believes that an action will benefit his beloved, he does not need to wonder whether there is a reason for him to perform it. Believing that the action will have that effect means that he already has a reason. Insofar as a person loves something, he necessarily counts its interests as giving him reasons to serve those interests. The fact that his beloved needs his help is in itself a reason for him to provide that help—a reason that takes precedence, other things being equal, over reasons for being comparably helpful to something that he does not love. That is part of what it means to love. Loving thus creates the reasons by which the lover's acts of devotion to his beloved are dictated and inspired.

13] Love entails two closely related volitional necessities. First, a person cannot help loving what he loves; and second, he therefore cannot help taking the expectation that an action would benefit his beloved as a powerful and often decisively preemptive reason for performing that action. Through loving, then, we acquire final ends to which we cannot help being bound; and by virtue of having those ends, we acquire reasons for acting that we cannot help but regard as particularly compelling.

It is not essential to love that it be accompanied by any particular feelings or thoughts. The heart of the matter is not affective or cognitive, but strictly volitional. The necessities of love, which drive our conduct and which circumscribe our options, are necessities of the will. Their grip means that there are certain considerations by which we cannot help

being moved to act, and which we cannot help counting
as reasons for action. What is essential to love is just these
constrained dispositions to reason and to act out of concern
for the beloved.

To be sure, the necessities that configure the lover's will
are often associated with extravagant passion, and also with
representations of the beloved as exceptionally worthy or
attractive. It is not difficult to understand why. Love commits
us to significant requirements and limitations. These are
boundaries that delineate the substance and the structure
of our wills. That is, they define what—as active beings—we
most intimately and essentially are. Accordingly, love is not
only risky. It profoundly shapes our personal identities and
the ways in which we experience our lives.

Therefore, it is only natural that loving tends to arouse
strong feelings in us. It is also only natural that we may hold
ourselves away from loving until we are satisfied that it will
be worth the anxieties, distractions, and other costs that it
is likely to bring. Thus, love is often accompanied both by
vivid enthusiasms and by reassuring characterizations of the
beloved. These may be very closely related to loving, but the
relationship is only contingent. They are not conceptually
indispensable elements of love.

14]   It is important to appreciate the difference between
the necessities of love and various other deeply entrenched
constraints upon the will, which are due to unwelcome and
more or less pathological conditions such as compulsions,
obsessions, and addictions. These conditions do not involve

what I understand by the term "volitional necessity." The necessities that they do involve may be even more urgent and more relentless than those of love; and their influence upon our lives may be no less pervasive and profound. However, they differ fundamentally from the volitional necessities of love in that we only submit to them unwillingly—that is, because they force us to do so. They are generated and sustained from outside the will itself. Their power over us is external and merely coercive. The power of love, on the other hand, is not like that.

Unfortunately, in attempting to explain the difference, it is easy to get lost in a thicket of complexities and qualifications. The trouble is that people are maddeningly nuanced and equivocal. It is impossible to grasp them accurately in their full depth and detail. They are too subtle, too fluid, and too mixed up for sharp and decisive analysis. So far as love is concerned, people tend to be so endlessly ambivalent and conflicted that it generally cannot be asserted entirely without caveat either that they do love something or that they don't. Frequently, the best that can be said is that part of them loves it and part of them does not.

In order to keep my discussion here fairly simple, I therefore propose just to stipulate that a lover is never troubled by conflict, or by ambivalence, or by any other sort of instability or confusion. Lovers do not waver or hold back. Their love, I shall assume, is always robustly wholehearted, uninhibited, and clear.

Now the necessities of wholehearted love may be irresistible, but they are not coercive. They do not prevail upon the lover against his will. On the contrary, they are constituted and confirmed by the fact that he cannot help being whole-heartedly behind them. The lover does not passively submit to the grip of love. He is fully identified with and responsible for its necessities. There is no distance or discrepancy between what a lover is constrained to will and what he cannot help wanting to will. The necessities of love are imposed upon him, then, by himself. It is by his own will that he does what they require. That is why love is not coercive. The lover may be unable to resist the power it exerts, but it is his own power.

Moreover, the wholehearted lover cannot help being wholehearted. His wholeheartedness is no more subject to the immediate control of his will than is his loving itself. There may be steps that would cause his love to falter and to fade; but someone whose love is genuinely wholehearted cannot bring himself to take those steps. He cannot deliberately try to stop himself from loving. His wholeheartedness means, by definition, that he has no reservations or conflicts that would move him to initiate or to support such an attempt. There is nothing within him that tends to undermine his love, or that gives him any interest in freeing himself from it. If the situation were otherwise, that would show either that his love had already somehow been undermined, or that it had never been truly wholehearted to begin with.

15]   The volitional necessities that I have been considering are absolute and unconditional. No rational person ever aims at death or disability or misery purely for their own sakes. In no possible circumstances could a rational person choose those things as final ends, or consider the likelihood that an action would achieve them as being in itself a reason for performing the action. Those judgments and choices are out of the question no matter what. They are precluded by volitional constraints that cannot be eluded and that never change.

Are these constraints "objective"? Well, in one sense they are obviously not objective. They derive from our attitudes; they are grounded nowhere but in the character of our own will. That evidently means that they are subjective. On the other hand, we cannot help having the dispositions that control the actions, choices, and reasons at issue. The character of our will could conceivably be different than it is. However, its actual contingent necessities are rigorous and stable; and they are outside our direct voluntary control. This warrants regarding them as objective, despite their origin within us.

It seems to me that what the principles of morality essentially accomplish is that they elaborate and elucidate universal and categorical necessities that constrain the human will. They develop a vision that inspires our love. Our moral ideals define certain qualities and conditions of life to which we are lovingly devoted. The point of the moral law is to codify how personal and social relationships must reasonably be ordered by people who cannot help caring about the final ends that are most fundamental in the lives of all fully rational beings.

It is sensible to insist that moral truths are, and must be,

stringently objective. After all, it would hardly do to suppose
that the requirements of morality depend upon what we
happen to want them to be, or upon what we happen to
think they are. So far as I can see, all the objectivity required
by the moral law is provided by the real necessities of our
volitionally rational will. There is no need to look elsewhere
to explain how moral judgments can be objective. In any case,
there is really nowhere else to look.

The truths of morality do not appear to be merely
contingent. The appearance that they are necessary truths
is, I believe, a reflection or a projection of the volitional
necessities from which morality derives. We are aware that we
have no choice, and we locate this inescapability in the object
instead of in its actual source, which is within ourselves. If we
suppose that the moral law is timeless and unalterable, that
is because we suppose—rightly or wrongly—that the most
fundamental volitional features of human nature are not
susceptible to change.

The particular mode of opprobrium that is characteristic
of our response to immorality is easy to account for when
we recognize that our moral beliefs promote a vision of ideal
personal and social relationships that has inspired our love.
Attributing moral blame is distinctively a way of being angry
at the wrongdoer. The anger is itself a kind of punishment.
This is perhaps most transparent when a person directs his
anger inward and suffers the lacerations of self-imposed
feelings of guilt. What makes moral anger understandable
and appropriate is that the transgression of an immoral
agent consists in his willfully rejecting and impeding the

realization of our moral ideal. In other words, he deliberately injures something that we love. That is enough to make anyone angry.

16]   Needless to say, many of our volitional necessities and final ends are far from universal. The fact that I care about various specific individuals, groups, and ways of doing things is not a function simply of generic human nature. It arises from my particular makeup and experience. Some of the things that I happen to love are also loved by others; but some of my loves are shared only by, at most, a small number of people. The very fact that these more personal volitional necessities are not universal implies that they depend upon variable conditions. Naturally, we cannot change them at will; but they can be changed. Even within the life of a single individual, love comes and it goes.

This certainly does not mean that loving one thing is as good as loving another. It is true that nothing is inherently either worthy or unworthy of being loved, independently of what we are and what we care about. The ground of normativity is relative in part to the common nature of human beings and in part to individual experience and character. Still, despite this relativity, there are plenty of ways that our loving can go absolutely wrong. There is plenty of room for demonstrating the seriousness of our normative discourse, in the way that counts so much for Adams and other normative realists, by "keeping an eye out for possible corrections of our views."

We may need to correct our views concerning what is

important to us because our love for one thing conflicts
with our love for another. Perhaps we care about worldly
success and also about peace of mind, and then it comes
to our attention that pursuing the one tends to interfere
with attaining the other. Determining which of the two
we love more is likely to be facilitated by increasing our
understanding of them. As we learn more about what each
is and what it entails, it will often become clear that one
arouses in us a more substantial interest and concern than
the other.

Even when we are not aware of any conflict among our
goals, it is only reasonable for us to be alert to the possibility
that we do not understand the people and the ideals and the
other things that we love well enough. Getting to know them
better may reveal conflicts that previously were unnoticed.
Our loving may turn out to have been misguided because
its objects are not what we thought they were, or because the
requirements and consequences of loving them differ from
what we had supposed. In love, no less than in other matters,
it is helpful to be clear about what we are getting into and
what that lets us in for.

In addition to the fact that our understanding of the
things we love may require correction, there is also the fact
that we often do not understand ourselves very well. It is
not so easy for people to know what they really care about or
what they truly love. Our motives and our dispositions are
notoriously uncertain and opaque, and we often get ourselves
wrong. It is hard to be sure what we can bring ourselves to do,
or how we will behave when the chips are down. The will is a

thing as real as any reality outside us. The truth about it does not depend upon what we think it is, or upon what we wish it were.

17]   Once we have learned as much as possible about the natural characteristics of the things we care about, and as much as possible about ourselves, there are no further substantive corrections that can be made. There is really nothing else to look for so far as the normativity of final ends is concerned. There is nothing else to get right.

The legitimacy and the worthiness of our final ends are not susceptible to being demonstrated by impersonal considerations that all rational agents would accept as appropriately controlling. Sometimes, normative disagreements cannot be rationally resolved. It may even be true that other people are required by what they care about to harm or to destroy what we love. Our love may be inspired by an endearing vision of how relationships between individuals might ideally be arranged; but other people may be driven by what they care about to struggle against arranging things in that way. There may be no convincing basis for regarding either them or ourselves as rationally defective or as having made some sort of mistake.

So far as reason goes, the conflict between us may be irreducible. There may be no way to deal with it, in the end, other than to separate or to slug it out. This is a discouraging outcome, but it does not imply a deficiency in my theory. It is just a fact of life.[5]

18]   Wholehearted love definitively settles, for each of us, issues
concerning what we are to care about. It expresses what we,
as active individuals, cannot help being. We have no recourse
other than to accept its dictates. Moreover, wholehearted love
expresses—beyond that—what we cannot help wholeheartedly wanting to be. This means that we accept its authority
as not merely inescapable, but as legitimate too. It is the only
legitimate authority upon which, for each of us, our normative attitudes and convictions can properly and finally rely.

Even after we have recognized what it is that we love and
acquiesced to it as establishing the defining necessities of
our volitional nature, problems do of course remain. We
can fail what we love, through ignorance or ineptitude; and
we can betray what we love, and thereby betray ourselves as
well, through a shallow indulgence that leads us to neglect its
interests and hence also to neglect our own. These problems
have to do with competence and character.

On the other hand, for normative guidance in understanding what we should want or what we should do, there
can be no authority superior to the welcome necessities of
our own nature. As in the realm of politics, the legitimacy of
authority here can derive only from the will of the governed.
A rational acquiescence to this authority requires a clear
self-understanding and a wholehearted acceptance of the
essential requirements and boundaries of our will. This
amounts to finding a mature confidence, which is not vulnerable to destruction of the self's integrity by familiar varieties
of hyperrationalistic skepticism.

This confidence, in which the authority of our norms of conduct are grounded, is a confidence in what we cannot help being. That provides us with the deepest and most secure foundation for practical reason. Without it, we could not even know where the exercise of practical rationality ought to begin. Without this confidence, in fact, there is no point in trying to become confident about anything else at all.[6]

Comments

Morality and the Logic of Caring

A Comment on Harry Frankfurt

CHRISTINE M. KORSGAARD

I agree with a great deal of what Harry Frankfurt has said in these lectures. I agree with Frankfurt's view that the distinguishing feature of human life is a form of self-consciousness—namely, our capacity to take our own mental states and activities as the objects of our attention (4–5). Like Frankfurt, I think that this form of self-consciousness is the source of the distinctively human tendency to self-assessment and the resulting capacity for normative self-government.[1] We also agree that this kind of self-consciousness is the source of normativity, or anyway makes normativity possible, and is the source of freedom of the will. Like Frankfurt, I reject the kind of normative realism which holds that (to use Frankfurt's own phrase), "volitional necessities are a response to an independent normative reality" (32). And like Frankfurt, I think that all normativity springs from the will.

But Frankfurt, if I understand him correctly, thinks that it follows from these views that the normativity of morality for any given agent is contingent on whether that agent cares about morality, or about the ideal of human relations that morality embodies (46–47).[2] And I don't agree with that. That is to say, I don't think that it *follows*, and I also don't think that it is true.[3] So in these comments I am going to discuss some ways in which I think a commitment to morality may be implied by what I will call the logic of caring.

Let me start by saying what I mean by that. As I just said, I believe that Frankfurt thinks that the dependence of normativity on caring simply implies that the normativity of morality for you depends on whether you happen to care about morality. It would imply that if the only kind of dependence that we allowed here was "being the direct object of caring." But this is not even Frankfurt's own view, for he thinks that caring about something can commit you to caring about other things. For instance, he says:

> When we do care about something, we go beyond wanting it. We want to go on wanting it, at least until the goal has been reached. Thus, we feel it as a lapse on our part if we neglect the desire, and we are disposed to take steps to refresh the desire if it should tend to fade. The caring entails, in other words, a commitment to the desire. (18–19)

I say that Frankfurt thinks that caring has a logic because Frankfurt thinks caring essentially implies—or *entails*, as he puts it—certain commitments that go beyond its immediate object. Caring about something entails that you continue to desire it, and this sets a standard that can motivate you to take corrective action should you "lapse" and fail to meet the standard.[4] In that sense caring is like believing or, in Kant's view, willing, both of which involve normative commitments that go beyond their immediate objects.[5] Believing, familiarly, commits you to the logical implications of whatever you believe. And according to Kant, willing an end commits you to willing the means to that end. This is because willing an end is determining yourself to be the cause of that end. And determining yourself to be the cause of something implies a commitment to using the available causal connections in order to achieve it—or in other words, to taking the means. Kant thinks that a commitment to taking the means to your ends is therefore constitutive of volition or willing. In the same way, Frankfurt thinks a commitment to continuing to desire x is constitutive of caring about x.

If caring in this way has a logic of its own, then the question about whether an agent is committed to morality by caring isn't settled by asking whether an agent happens to care directly about morality. We must also ask whether the agent's cares and loves might commit him, by virtue of other features of the logic of caring, to moral values and principles.[6]

Before I talk about that possibility, however, I want to notice certain differences between my own Kantian views and Frankfurt's that may be relevant to the argument that I am about to make. Frankfurt thinks of reason and the will as separate faculties—he tells us that "the ultimate source of practical normative authority lies not in reason but in the will" (3). By contrast, I follow Kant in thinking that, at least in human beings, practical reason is the will, in the sense that the principles of practical reason are constitutive of volition.

I have already explained why I think that the hypothetical imperative, which instructs us to take the means to our ends, is constitutive of volition; and below I will explain why I think that a formal version of the categorical imperative, which instructs us to will our maxims as universal laws, is also constitutive of volition. A related difference is that, on the Kantian view, self-consciousness is the direct source of reason, and of itself places us under the normative authority of the principles of reason. When a human being is inclined to act in a certain way for the sake of a certain end, he is conscious of these facts about himself, and this not only enables but requires him to ask himself whether he should act in the way he is inclined to. On Kant's view, this amounts to asking whether the maxim of performing that act for the sake that end can serve as a normative principle for the will, and that, for reasons I will mention shortly, is in turn a question about whether that maxim can serve as a universal law. If these arguments work, then the very fact of being self-conscious places us directly under the normative authority of the principles of practical reason.[7]

Frankfurt, by contrast, thinks that the authority of practical reason "is grounded in and derives from the authority of love" (3).[8] However, this is not quite as straightforward a disagreement as it seems, because Frankfurt has a different view of practical reason from the Kantian one I just described. On the Kantian view, the principles of practical reason are the categorical and hypothetical imperatives, and the categorical imperative is of course supposed to be identical to the moral law. By contrast, in his first lecture, when

Frankfurt denies that the normative authority of morality can be grounded in reason, he identifies reason simply with the avoidance of contradictions and fallacies. Despite Frankfurt's invocation of Thomas Nagel in his first lecture (33), Frankfurt does not seem to have a specifically practical form of reason, such as that represented by the Kantian imperatives, in mind (21–22).[9] Similarly, in his second lecture, Frankfurt identifies "formal rationality" with the truths of logic, again apparently, although not explicitly, denying that there are formal principles that are specific to practical reason. Yet Frankfurt evidently thinks that practical reason does include the hypothetical imperative or principle of instrumental reason, for he says that "practical reasoning is, in part, a procedure through which we determine what we have most reason to do in order to reach our goals" (13). It is not clear to me whether he considers this part of formal reason or of what he calls "volitional rationality" (31), which is grounded in love. Certainly, there is a sense in which one might argue that the authority of particular instrumental requirements is grounded in love. I have myself argued elsewhere that we can be under a rational obligation to take the means to an end only if the end itself has normative authority.[10] We cannot be under a rational obligation to take the means to an end if the end is merely the object of a desire. Because Frankfurt also thinks that desires are not in and of themselves authoritative (18), but rather are rendered normative by love or caring, perhaps he too thinks that in that sense the authority of instrumental reason depends upon love. Only ends we love or care about can give rise to instrumental reasons. What he says about instrumental reason in his first lecture suggests this view (20–24). But the *formal* principle of instrumental reason (as opposed to particular instrumental requirements) still seems to me to depend on the way it is constitutive of volition. In any case, when he talks about practical reason Frankfurt is referring to his category of "volitional rationality."[11] As far as I can see, it is only this kind of rationality that Frankfurt thinks is grounded in love or caring. So whether we are disagreeing about the ground of the authority of practical reason or about the nature of practical reason is a little unclear.

Despite this possible disagreement, there is an important similarity between Frankfurt's view of caring and my own view of practical reason, which I want to describe for two reasons—first, because it presents a problem, which I think Frankfurt needs to address in any case; and second, because on my own view the solution to that problem suggests one way that a commitment to morality might be entailed by caring (or, as I would prefer to say, by willing). After the passage in which he says that caring about x entails a commitment to continuing to desire x, Frankfurt continues:

> Willing freely means that the self is at that time harmoniously integrated. There is, within it, a synchronic coherence. Caring about something implies a diachronic coherence, which integrates the self across time. . . . By our caring, . . . we engage ourselves in guiding the course of our desires. If we cared about nothing, we would play no active role in designing the successive configurations of our will. (19)

Frankfurt thinks that caring is constitutive of the unity (or

at least of the diachronic unity) of the will or the self. I hold
a similar view about acts of rational willing as Kant understands them—acts of will that conform to the principles of
practical reason. To support the comparison I am about to
make, I need first to explain why I think that the unity of the
will or the self depends on a formal version of the categorical
imperative, the principle that our maxims must be willed as
universal laws. So I am going to ask your patience during a
slight excursion into Kantian philosophy whose relevance to
Frankfurt will only become clear later on. This will also serve
to help explain why I think we are under the authority of
practical reason, with or without love.

Suppose I decide to go to the dentist on a certain day in
order to get a cavity filled. I think I have a reason to do this.
As Kant would put it, I think that a certain maxim—roughly,
the maxim of going to the dentist in order to get a cavity
filled—embodies a reason. When I make this my maxim, my
commitment is universal in the following sense: I commit
myself to acting as this maxim specifies—going to the dentist
on the occasion of my appointment—in all circumstances
that are relevantly similar to the ones I expect to obtain at
the time of my appointment, by which I mean, going when
the time comes, so long as I still have both the cavity and the
appointment, and unless there is a good reason why not. The
universality holds over all relevantly similar circumstances
in the sense that if there is good reason not to go when the
time comes, the circumstances must be relevantly dissimilar
to the ones I expected. Now it may turn out through some
extraordinary circumstance that in order to get to the dentist

on time on the occasion of my appointment, I have to risk
my life. (Perhaps a terrorist claims to have planted a bomb on
the bus I would have to take in order to get there.) Because
there is good reason not to risk my life for the sake of a
filling, I can give up the project of going to the dentist on the
occasion of my appointment without violating the universality of my maxim, because my maxim says to act a certain way
unless there is good reason why not. On the other hand, it
may be that I am really terrified of the dentist and therefore
I am *always* tempted to find some excuse not to go when the
day arrives. Now if I am prepared to give up the project of
going to the dentist in the face of *any consideration whatever*
that tempts me to do so—that is, if I am prepared to count
any desire or temptation as a good reason not to go (and so
any circumstance as "relevantly dissimilar"), then clearly I
have not really committed myself to anything. But if I have
not really committed myself to anything, then I have not
really willed anything. I am just going to do whatever my
desire prompts me to do at the moment of action regardless,
and my will is not operative. So in order to avoid being what
Frankfurt calls a wanton, who follows every desire that comes
along, I have to will my maxim as a universal law. That is, I
have to will it as a law that has some universal force—a law
that is to be acted on in all relevantly similar circumstances,
or unless there is some good reason why not. So I must will
a maxim that is in some sense universal in order to will
anything at all. And that means that if my maxim cannot be
universal, I cannot will it. Therefore I am under a universalizability requirement.[12]

Now if Kant himself is right, there is a short route from here to a commitment to morality, because Kant apparently thinks that a commitment to this kind of formal universalizability just is a commitment to the moral law. But it looks as if it is not going to be quite that easy, because the moral law is not just a formal principle of universalizability, but rather a principle that demands that we will a maxim that universalizes over all rational agents.[13] And even if we suppose that we must universalize over all rational agents, a commitment to universalization gets us into moral territory only on the assumption that reasons have what I have elsewhere called a "public" or essentially intersubjective or agent-neutral normative force.

To see why, suppose I ask whether a certain maxim can serve as a universal law. Take it for now that the first problem is solved, so that what I am asking is whether it can be a universal law for all rational agents. For instance, we agree that I cannot will the maxim of "stealing a certain object just because I want it" as a universal law unless I can will that any rational being who wants an object should steal it. What kind of limitation does this impose? If practical reasons are private or agent-relative, it commits me only to acknowledging that if my desire for an object is a good reason for me to steal it, then your desire for an object is a good reason for you to steal it. It does not give me any reason to promote the satisfaction of your desire.

If practical reasons are public, however, it must be possible for us to share them—that is, to share in their normative force. Any reasons that I assign to you must also be ones that I can share with you and can take to have normative force for me. In that case, I cannot will to steal an object from you unless I could possibly will that you *should* in similar circumstances steal the object from me. Assuming that I cannot do that, consistent with my end of possessing the object, I find that I cannot will this maxim as a universal law.[14] And therefore I conclude that my wanting something cannot provide a sufficient reason for stealing it. So if the universal law universalizes over all rational beings and yields public reasons, then it turns out to be something like Kant's moral law.

But what, if anything, compels us to view reasons as public and universal in this way?[15] In my view, part of the answer lies in the role of universal principles in unifying and therefore constituting the will or the self, the role played in Frankfurt's view by caring. And if the self is constituted by volition, it cannot be assumed to exist in advance of volition. When I will to go to the dentist on the day of my appointment, I cannot be willing a law that *my future self* should go to the dentist, for whether I *have* a future self depends on whether that law and others like it are obeyed. If that law and others like it are not obeyed, then my body is, in Frankfurt's terms, not that of a person but that of a wanton without a self, and no person has disobeyed my law. So I must be willing that an agent characterized in some other way—perhaps as the future conscious subject of my body—should go to the dentist. Minimally, this shows that any maxim that I will must universalize over *some* group more inclusive than my present conscious self, and that the normative force of the reason I legislate should be public and shared between me (my present conscious self) and the members of that group.[16] Perhaps it is only all the future conscious subjects of my body, but we need some reason why that and only that should be the relevant group, and some of the possible answers to that question suggest that the group should be more inclusive still. For instance, one possible answer is that I must interact cooperatively with the future conscious subjects of my body if I am to carry any of my projects out. But of course it may also be argued that I must interact cooperatively with other rational agents as well, for unless others respect my reasons and I respect theirs, we are apt to get in each other's way.[17] So it begins to look as if I must will universally and pub-licly—that is, will reasons I can share, not only with the future conscious subjects of my body, but with all rational beings, or at least all with whom I must interact. In any case, I cannot coherently regard my reasons as applying merely to myself. And there may be the beginnings of a route to morality.

That obviously is not a complete argument but rather only a tentative sketch for one, and I am not going to carry it any further here.[18] I mention it only because Frankfurt's view of the role of caring in integrating the self is very much like my view of the role of the principles of practical reason in integrating the self, and so I think his view faces a problem like the one I just described. If continuing to desire the things that you care about is constitutive of the (diachronic) self, the norm of continuing to desire the things that you care about cannot simply be addressed to the self, because whether you have a (diachronic) self depends on whether that norm is obeyed. So to whom is it addressed? Frankfurt apparently wants to hold both that my carings are normative for me alone and that my will is constituted by my carings. I do not see how to make these views consistent—or rather, I think more needs to be said. If Frankfurt thinks that the norm of continuing to desire the things I care about is addressed to the future conscious subjects of my body, then Frankfurt is at once assuming both that personal identity is constituted by bodily continuity and that personal identity is constituted by acts of caring. He needs to say why and how these things work together. If he grants that the norm of continuing to desire the things that I care about must be public and universal between me and some group of my interactive partners, as I have tentatively suggested, perhaps he too is on the road to morality after all.

I have just been comparing the role that Frankfurt gives to caring in unifying the self with the role that I believe the principles of practical reason play in unifying the self. I have been suggesting that perhaps in both cases the unifying factor—the norm of caring or practical principles—cannot successfully unify the self unless it is interpreted in a way that implies a commitment to morality, or at least to the public normative force of reasons. A commitment to continuing to desire what I care about implies that my future self—another self—should care about the same thing I do. Having made this comparison, I would like to mention some disanalogies between our two views that I believe give rise to further questions. As I have indicated above, I think that we can explain *why* the principles of practical reason are constitutive of volition and agency.[19] So here is a question for Frankfurt:

why is continuing to desire x constitutive of caring about x? Continuing to care may be constitutive of the self that does the caring, but why does that self need to be unified in order to care? In my own view, a person needs to be unified insofar as she is an agent, because it is one of the distinguishing features of action that a movement only counts as an action if it is caused by the person considered as a whole, rather than by a part of her.[20] The principles of practical reason must secure the unity of the self because they are constitutive of volition and so of agency, and agency must be unified. I am not sure whether this answer is available to Frankfurt or not, in part because I am uncertain how exactly he understands the will.

Although Frankfurt describes caring as part of the will, as far as I can see, it merely informs volition and is not really constitutive of it. Caring about something is not the same as acting from that concern, while, I believe, willing a universal maxim is the same as acting on that maxim.[21] Despite his characterization of caring as a feature of the will, Frankfurt sometimes seems to think that the will is just the desire you act on. For instance, he says that we will freely "when the will behind what we do is exactly the will by which we want our action to be moved" (15). On another occasion, however, he claims that if desires we reject "succeed in moving us to act, it will now be only against our will" (7), suggesting a difference between your will and the desire that produces your action. (Perhaps Frankfurt thinks we sometimes act from a will that is not our own, and that is what is behind the careful formulation "the will behind what we do" in the first of those remarks.)

Some of these remarks suggest that Frankfurt holds the

view that an action is a movement caused by a desire. On this view, a wanton would count as having a will and as being an agent, even though the wanton would not be a person and would be neither free nor unfree. I do not think that this is correct. An action is not a movement caused by a desire: the idea of action requires that the agent *take* the desire to make the movement appropriate. In the case of adult human agents, this means that the agent takes the desire to provide a reason for the movement. That "taking" represents the agent's principle, so that action always involves a principle: if I take my desire for x to be a reason for doing y, my principle—or maxim—is one of doing y for the sake of x. Wantonness in Frankfurt's sense—unprincipled action—is, on my view, excluded by the concept of action. One might have a principle of doing whatever one desires, but that is not wantonness in Frankfurt's sense. Frankfurt thinks nonhuman animals are wantons, but on my view, nonhuman agents—for, like Frankfurt, I think that nonhuman animals may be agents—cannot be. Rather, their instincts must be understood as presenting certain situations as appropriate grounds for making certain movements, and therefore as serving as their principles.[22] In any case, I think the will cannot be identified with the desire you act on (or any other desire): the will must be constituted by its principles. And in constituting the will, these principles must give the will the unity that makes agency possible. I believe that for Frankfurt to take the position that caring is constitutive of the self because caring unifies the self, he either needs to make caring constitutive of agency, or he needs some other account of why the self should be unified.

I now want to leave these rather metaphysical (and no doubt obscure) arguments aside and turn to another, simpler, way in which a commitment to morality may be entailed by caring. If something like the view I just sketched is right, it leaves us with a problem, which I am going to call the problem of the personal. If reasons are, as I have suggested, public and universal for all rational beings, then anyone's reasons are reasons for me. What then entitles me to pay special attention to what I will call "my own reasons"—that is, reasons whose first origin lies in my own desires and interests, or in the desires and interests of the people about whom I care most? Utilitarians, familiarly, handle this problem by making claims about how to efficiently maximize utility. They claim that I am obligated to treat everyone's reasons as equally important, and so to add them all up in a single calculation, and do what promotes the best result overall. But tradition- ally they also claim that it turns out, happily, that I can best promote the overall total by attending most directly to my own projects and to the interests and concerns of my loved ones. This theory has been criticized for offering us the right conclusion for the wrong reason, both theoretically and for agents themselves. As Bernard Williams has argued, it is not possible for agents to favor their own projects or loved ones both from a direct personal commitment and because this is the most efficient way to maximize utility.[23]

Those of us who do not believe it makes sense to add values across the boundaries between persons do not face the problem in the exact form that utilitarians do. Yet there certainly is a problem here. Why exactly am I to be permitted to give my own projects and interests and those of my loved ones the preference over other people's? How can I square this with my commitment to the view that in some sense their projects and interests are just as important as mine? What we seem to want here is a theory that

    1. Allows us to actively devote our lives to promoting our own projects and the concerns of those we care about, and not everyone's.

    2. Requires us to concede that the projects and loved ones of strangers are just as important as our own.

    3. Requires us to refrain in certain ways from damaging or hindering other people's interests, even those we are not required to promote them.

    4. Requires us to help others to satisfy certain of their most basic needs even though we are not required to promote their interests as directly and vigorously as our own.

It is surprisingly difficulty to come up with a philosophical theory that manages all of this at once.[24] Frankfurt's solution is to make a distinction between what is of value and what one cares about or loves. He says:

> From the fact that we consider something to be valuable, it does not follow that we need to be concerned with it. There are many objects, activities, and states of affairs that we acknowledge to be valuable but in which we quite reasonably take no interest because they do not fit into our lives. Other things, perhaps even of lesser value, are more important to us. What we are actually to care about—what we are to regard as really important to us—cannot be based simply upon judgments concerning what has the most value. (27–28)

Frankfurt thinks it is only the things that we care about that give us reasons to act. In principle, this goes to a kind of opposite extreme from utilitarianism: in Frankfurt's view, we have no reason to be attentive to the good of others at all, unless we happen to care, either about those specific others, or about the general ideal of human relationships embodied in morality.

As an aside, I should note that it is a little unclear to me what Frankfurt means when he talks about something's being "valuable," and also when he talks about something being "more valuable." It is evident from what he says that these are not directly normative judgments for Frankfurt. Perhaps he thinks they are simply judgments about real values, but it seems a shame to go to all the trouble to deny normative realism about values and then espouse a kind of nonnormative realism about them after all. Or perhaps what he means when he calls something valuable is that someone does love or care about it, or that it is the sort of thing that it is somehow appropriate for people to love or care about.[25] Frankfurt's characterization of certain preferences and loves as "crazy" or "lunatic" or "inhuman" (29) suggests that he accepts the existence of such standards. When Frankfurt suggests that I might acknowledge that something is "more valuable" than the things I care most about, perhaps he means I might acknowledge that they are of deeper and greater concern to other people—or maybe large numbers of other people—than the thing I care about is to me.

However that may be, I don't think Frankfurt's solution to the problem is right. To some extent, I agree with him about the phenomena. I care deeply about finishing my next book, and will devote a kind of effort to it that I will not devote to helping to stop the spread of AIDS in Africa, even though I agree that the latter is a far more important and valuable project. It does not, in Frankfurt's words, fit into my life in the same way. But this kind of example doesn't make me want to accept Frankfurt's view, for a couple of reasons. First, I think that acknowledging the value of other projects puts a check on the kinds of reasons I can derive from my own projects, even where those other projects are not among the things I particularly care about. Suppose that through some bizarre concatenation of circumstances, my writing my book would make the African AIDS epidemic worse. Heaven only knows what it would be, but philosophers can always think of something. So: Suppose that I am the carrier of a virus that is harmless to me, but that would seriously sicken people with compromised immune systems. And suppose in order to finish my book I need to go on a research trip to Africa in order to consult a manuscript that St. Augustine left there and that may not be copied or moved. If I insisted on going, knowing that a large number of people would become deathly ill as a result of exposure to me, it seems to me that this choice would be, to use Frankfurt's words, "crazy," "lunatic," and "inhuman." But this isn't merely because, as it happens, I am a person who cares about morality. I think there would be something wrong not just with me and my character and my attitude towards the people in Africa, but with my attitude towards *writing the book*, if I cared about it in this way. Furthermore, I do not think this is just because writing a book is usually comparatively less important than saving lives. Suppose the question concerns what I would do to save the life of my child. No doubt if I had a child, I would do things to save the life of that child that I would not do to save the life of other people's children—not even to save the lives of many other people's children. But—and here I am borrowing a point from Tim Scanlon—I think that if I were prepared to kill other people's children to get their organs in order to save the life of my child, that would reveal something amiss, not merely with my general moral character and my attitude towards the other children, but with my attitude toward my own child.[26] As Scanlon puts it, it would be as if I felt that my child's right to her own organs derived from my love for her, and that would be the wrong way of caring about her.[27] And this is the second point: that the kind of value we assign to something or someone that we care about naturally generalizes in a certain way.

Elsewhere I have proposed a different model for understanding the relation between universal values and personal projects.[28] I believe instead of thinking of personal projects as arising from specific or personal values, we should think of them as arising from a desire to stand in a special relationship to something that we regard as having intersubjective or universal value. Love, as I understand it, would be an example of this. When I love, say, a person, I regard his humanity—his autonomy and his interests—as something of universal and public value. These are values that I think everyone has reason to respect and perhaps even some reason to promote. But I also desire to stand in a special relation to him and to those values: I want to share in his life and his decisions and if it is possible to be the one who promotes his good. I do not want this, as the utilitarian would have it, merely because it is the way I can most effectively promote the sum total of value, but because it is something of special concern to myself— perhaps something that is essential to my practical identity. Nevertheless, any reasons that spring from this desire are essentially limited by the values to which I want to stand in a special relation. So although I would prefer to be the one who makes my beloved happy, I cannot therefore conclude I have a reason to try to prevent someone else from making him happy, or to undercut his autonomy by trying to prevent him from consorting with his other friends. My reasons must be essentially respectful of the kind of value I accord to him, which is the value of his humanity, and requires respect for his autonomy and his good.

Frankfurt's conception of love, by contrast to the attitude I am trying to describe, seems both too personal and too impersonal. Frankfurt's description of what the lover wants is too impersonal. He says that love is a concern for the existence and the good of what is loved, that the lover accepts the interests of the beloved as his own, and that "love does not necessarily include a desire for union of any other kind" (41). This just doesn't ring true to me. My love for my friends and family includes a desire to share my life with them; my love for philosophy includes a desire to do it and to succeed at it. I do not merely care for its existence and its good. One way to put the point: if my loves are to give my life meaning, as Frankfurt thinks they do, they must give me something to do, not just something to root for. But as I have suggested, the reasons I derive from my desire to stand in a special relation to my beloved must be conditioned by a concern for its existence and its good. Indeed, it is one of the recognizable pathologies of love when it is not. The jealous lover who is prepared to kill his beloved rather than let her be with anyone else, the literary plagiarist, or the scientist who fakes his data—all of these people let their desires to stand in a special relation to something that is of value get the better of their desire to serve the value itself. But the reason why these are such recognizable pathologies is because love is not as disinterested as Frankfurt thinks. Even the love of a parent for a child, which I believe is Frankfurt's model, characteristically involves a desire to be the one who helps and nurtures the child, where that is possible and not against the interests of the child. I do not think that love's wishes are, or even should be, as impersonal and unselfish as Frankfurt describes them.

But in another way Frankfurt's conception of love and personal value is too personal. I agree with Frankfurt that love is not, or not necessarily, a response to value, that its object is particular and its causes multifarious. Because there are many things of value, your wanting to stand in a special relationship to one of them is clearly not caused merely by the fact that you see it as of value. Yet I think that in loving something you do accord universal or public value to its object.[29] And I think that someone who loves something with a certain kind of value is committed to that kind of value in general. As the case of stealing the organs shows, if I am to be respectful of the value of humanity in my beloved, then

I must be respectful of that value generally. This, I think, is why people are inclined to think that love is—to put it in a slightly old-fashioned way—redemptive, why even though love is not the same thing as morality, it tends to make us better. And that is another way in which moral commitment may be entailed by the logic of caring.[30]

Let me conclude by summing up the points I have made. First, I have argued that it does not follow from the fact that all normativity arises from caring, if that is a fact, that the normativity of morality depends only on whether one contingently cares about it. Caring has a logic of its own, and it may be that caring about things in general commits one to morality. Second, I have sketched two ways that one might argue for such an implication. First, I have suggested that caring cannot fulfill its role in constituting personal identity unless the reasons to which it gives rise are to some extent regarded as universal and public by the person who has them. Second, I have suggested that caring about something essentially involves according it a kind of universal and public value, even though I agree with Frankfurt that love is not merely a response to that kind of value. Respecting that value as you find it in your beloved commits you to respecting it wherever you find it. In both of these ways, it is possible that the logic of caring commits us to universal shared values, and so to morality.

A Thoughtful and Reasonable Stability

A Comment on Harry Frankfurt's 2004 Tanner Lectures

MICHAEL E. BRATMAN

"What a person really needs to know, in order to know how to live," Harry G. Frankfurt tells us in Lecture Two, "is what to care about and how to measure the relative importance to him of the various things about which he cares." A solution provides us with "an organized repertoire of final ends. That puts us in a position to determine, both in general and in particular instances, what we have reason to do" (28).

It is a mistake, according to Frankfurt, to think that we can achieve a solution simply by reflection on what is of value or on what morality requires: "Neither . . . can settle this for you," he tells us (28). Not just anything goes, however. A solution is significantly constrained by certain "volitional necessities"—certain things about which we cannot help but to care, when this incapacity is itself one that we "cannot help being wholeheartedly behind" (45). Very roughly, if caring for x is volitionally necessary for you, it is not in your power to give it up at will, it is not in your power to change this fact about yourself at will, and you wholeheartedly—that is, without relevant ambivalence on your part—favor all this.

Volitionally necessary caring comes in two forms. There are "fundamental necessities" that "are solidly entrenched in our human nature" in ways that probably have an evolutionary explanation. Examples include our love for "being intact and healthy, being satisfied, and being in touch" (38). Second, there are person-specific volitional necessities—a person's love for a particular person or ideal, for example. Each case is to be distinguished from the volitional incapacity of the unwilling addict who does not wholeheartedly favor his incapacity. Love is not addiction.

As I understand him—though I am unsure—Frankfurt supposes that the fundamental necessities to which he alludes are volitional necessities in the sense that involves wholehearted support. Our inescapable concern for our own survival is accompanied by our inescapable wholehearted support for having this inescapable concern to survive. There is a certain optimism here.

A central case of volitionally necessary caring is love, according to Frankfurt. Love can be a fundamental necessity, as in our love of life; or it can be a person-specific necessity as in one's love for a particular person or ideal. Whereas fundamental necessities are ones we simply cannot give up, period, it may be possible to give up a person-specific necessity over time: we do fall out of love. But giving it up right now, at will, is not in our power.

As Frankfurt sees it, love is "a powerful source of reasons" (42). "Insofar as a person loves something, he necessarily counts its interests as giving him reasons to serve those interests" (42). Love provides us with "final ends to which we cannot help being bound; and by virtue of having those ends, we acquire reasons for acting that we cannot help but regard as particularly compelling" (42).

It is to the volitional necessities of love that we should look if we want to find the form of objectivity that is relevant to practical thought. Indeed, "all the objectivity required by the moral law is provided by the real necessities of our volitionally rational will" (47). And a recognition of these volitional necessities can ground a "mature confidence" in our practical thinking and agency, a mature "confidence in what we cannot help being" (52). In these ways, the concern with "getting it right" is answered by an appeal to "what we cannot help being."

This is powerful and exciting philosophy. It shows, once again, the philosophical depth and fecundity of the project—begun over thirty years ago with the publication of "Freedom of the Will and the Concept of a Person"—of reconceptualizing the basic framework at work in our understanding of human agency and, as Frankfurt says, the structure of a person's will. You gotta love it. Nevertheless, I do worry about several points.

Begin with the limits of value judgment and of moral judgment. Frankfurt indicates that these underdetermine a person's sensible answer to the question of how to live. And this seems true and important. There are just too many goods and not enough time, so to speak. Even once we have in some way built a certain good into our lives, there remain issues of how important it is to be; and here again, judgments about value are likely to underdetermine. Moral judgment—understood by Frankfurt as concerned with our relations to others—provides, at most, certain constraints rather than a full-blown answer to Frankfurt's question about how to live.

It does not follow from this, though, that in figuring out how to live, value judgment and moral judgment have no roles to play. Value judgment and moral judgment might underdetermine how to live, but still impose constraints on an answer to the question of how to live. Frankfurt does not tell us much about how he is understanding value judgments or about how we can perhaps come to know them, though he is clearly willing to make them. But he does indicate that morality "derives" from certain "volitional necessities" (46). So morality—or anyway its purported basis—does constrain how to live by making certain ways of living volitionally impossible for us.

There are two ideas here. First, there is the idea that insofar as morality involves a kind of inescapability or necessity, this is a necessity not of rationality but of the will. The second idea is that morality "derives" from these necessities. Which necessities? Here I find myself in need of clarification. On the one hand, "fundamental" necessities seem rather thin: even if our love for our own survival is a universal necessity, love for the survival of others seems, I am sad to say, rather less universally present.[1] On the other hand, person-specific volitional necessities, in the form of, as Frankfurt says, love for certain "ideal personal and social relationships" (47), can help explain, as Frankfurt emphasizes, the special force of the moral reactive emotions, like moral anger and guilt. But this seems to give up the idea that, as Frankfurt says, "the principles of morality . . . elucidate universal and categorical necessities that constrain the human will" (46). I also wonder whether such moral ideals really are, typically, volitionally necessary in Frankfurt's sense, rather than revisable, even if wholehearted and psychologically entrenched and stable, commitments. Although my condemnation of torturing children may well be volitionally necessary for me, my moral commitment to, say, a form of pacifism, or to political liberalism, may be wholehearted and settled without involving an incapacity to change.

Granted, my commitment to a moral ideal will itself constrain what else is volitionally possible for me, and what else I treat as a reason. It will anchor certain derivative necessities of the will. But it does not follow that my commitment is itself volitionally necessary, or that it needs to be volitionally necessary to help explain the moral reactive emotions.

Love is a source of reasons, according to Frankfurt. Frankfurt associates this claim with the idea that love necessarily involves counting or treating certain things as reasons for action. I agree with this connection between love and treating as a reason. But this does raise the question of whether what we love could be so bad—indeed, in other work Frankfurt has specifically noted the possibility of wholeheartedly loving "what is bad, or what is evil"[2]—that, though we are thereby set to *treat* it as a reason, it is not a reason.

Perhaps Jones wholeheartedly cares about and pursues revenge. Perhaps he loves revenge. Such wholehearted caring or love involves treating relevant considerations as reasons. But it seems that we may well also have the critical thought— one that it might be important to us to be able to express to Jones and to others—that he has not got it right, that revenge and its love and pursuit are very bad things, and so the love for revenge does not provide a reason.[3] It seems that we can have this critical thought while recognizing that Jones will, as part of his wholehearted caring or love, treat revenge as a reason, and that he would indeed be internally incoherent to continue so to care or to love, but not to treat it as a reason.

As noted, Frankfurt is quite willing to make judgments of the goodness or badness of what is loved and of loving it. So there is a live question for his theory of how to put together judgments of reasons for action with judgments of value. Frankfurt's own official answer to this question is that love for what is bad or evil does provide a reason for action. He asks, "When does a fact give us a reason for performing an action?" He then answers himself: "When it suggests that performing the action would help us reach one or another of our goals" (11). Frankfurt emphasizes that not all desires are goals in the relevant sense; but Jones's wholehearted commitment to revenge is, I take it, a goal in Frankfurt's sense. And this purported sufficient condition for a reason for action does not include any condition on the value of one's goal.

It does seem to me, though, that Frankfurt's central

insights about the significance of caring, wholeheartedness, and love to our agency may be available to a theory that gives a somewhat different answer to this question of the relation between reasons for action and value. Suppose we grant, with Frankfurt, that value judgments underdetermine how to live, and that what we care about "is the ultimate touchstone and basis of our practical reasoning" (28) in the sense that our practical reasoning needs to be grounded in what we love or care about. Simply thinking something good is not yet a sufficient ground for practical reasoning that leads to action that matters to us, because we still may not care about it. Further, when we do care about or love something, this may not be explained by a judgment on our part that it is a good thing. All this, however, leaves open the critical thought that in certain cases, caring about or loving something that is bad or evil does not provide a reason for action, even though it does exert rational pressures of coherence in the direction of treating relevant considerations as reasons.

Frankfurt also holds that love is an essential element of the "inner harmony" that constitutes "contentment or self-esteem" and that this inner harmony is a "very good thing" (17). And he holds that there can be this inner harmony even in the life of a bad person. As he says elsewhere, "Being wholehearted is quite compatible . . . with being dreadfully and irredeemably wicked."[4] This may suggest something like the following argument: Contentment is a very good thing; love is necessary for contentment; treating what one loves as a reason for action is a necessary condition of loving it; so treating what one loves as a reason for action is a necessary condition of contentment, which is a very good thing. So what one loves is a reason for action even if what one loves is bad or evil. However, this conclusion does not follow. Perhaps in some cases this very good thing of contentment or "inner harmony" involves treating as a reason something that is not. This may be the case when—to invert the more common worry—this very good thing happens to bad people.

Put it this way: Two theses that are central to Frankfurt's theory are, first, that the psychological functioning characteristic of inner harmony involves treating what one loves as a reason, and second, that there can be this harmony even if what one loves is bad or evil. A broadly Frankfurtian theory could hold both these views and still go on to say (though Frankfurt does not) that our talk of reasons—that is, our talk of normative reasons—has two faces: it tracks such functioning, and it tracks judgments of value. If we were to take such a view, we would then be in a position to say that, in certain cases, love for what is bad does not suffice for reasons.

Frankfurt tells us that a solution to the problem of how to live provides "an organized repertoire of final ends" (28). Frankfurt sometimes suggests that these final ends must be things that we love, and so must be volitionally necessary. But he sometimes suggests that they can include things we care about but do not, strictly speaking, love (because our caring is not volitionally necessary). It is this latter view that seems right to me: finality of end is not the same as necessity of end. Wholehearted caring need not be volitionally necessary to specify a person's final ends. I can wholeheartedly care about a life of scholarship, or a life that conforms to the religious traditions of my ancestors, or a life of political activism, or a life of intense sexuality, while retaining the ability to give these things up. Of course, in being whole-hearted about, say, scholarship, I have no intention at all to give it up, and I think it is a good and morally permissible life, and one that I find rewarding. But that does not mean I am *incapable* of giving it up. Wholeheartedness and the absence of any intention to change need not involve an incapacity. That I quite sensibly *would* not change does not mean that I *could* not change. I may stand in a different relation to where I stand than Martin Luther famously thought that he did.

It seems to me, then, that deeply entrenched but nonvoli-tionally necessary carings about which we are wholehearted suffice to provide a person's final ends. In saying this, I mean to leave it open how exactly to understand caring. I myself would be inclined to think of caring as involving a settled intention-like commitment to treating certain consider-ations as justifying. Frankfurt points to a model of caring as a hierarchical structure of desire. And other views are possible. The present point does not address this debate. It says only that caring can be wholehearted and can specify a person's final ends, without being volitionally necessary.

The things I wholeheartedly care about are, I think it is plausible to say, like planks in Neurath's famous boat. In practical reflection, I cannot sensibly step back from all of them at once and ask—from no standpoint in particular—what to do. I need to start from some planks or other. I cannot, as Frankfurt says in his first lecture, pull myself up by my own bootstraps (24). But substantive and determinate planks need not themselves be volitionally necessary, though they may. From "I can't reflect without standing on some plank or other," we cannot infer "there is some plank on which I must stand." Perhaps a complex of wholehearted cares and concerns, no one of which is volitionally necessary but all of which have survived or would survive reflection from the standpoint of other basic "planks," would be enough to provide for a "mature confidence" in how I am living my life.

I do not say there are no volitional necessities in Frankfurt's sense. I just want to put them in their place. Though we do not have in these lectures a full account of just what such necessity is, we can agree with Frankfurt that there is an important sense in which, for example, we are volitionally incapable of not caring at all about our own survival, and that most parents are volitionally incapable of not caring about their young children. But what is the role of these necessities in answering the question of how to live? I find it plausible that they provide background constraints, but that they significantly underdetermine our answers to this question. They do not "settle" how to live any more than does value judgment.

Further, it is not clear to me that what volitional necessities there are play as preemptive a role as Frankfurt suggests. Frankfurt says that love gives us "reasons for acting that we cannot help but regard as particularly compelling." Putting aside worries about love for what is bad, this remark is supported by Frankfurt's account when we understand "particularly compelling" as meaning unavoidable. However, it also seems to be Frankfurt's view that reasons of love are, as well, particularly weighty or preemptive. But once we note the potential role of nonnecessary carings, we can see that this does not follow, and may not be true. Perhaps wholehearted carings that are not volitionally necessary can provide reasons that outweigh those of love. Volitional necessity need not ensure overriding justifying significance.

A sufficiently determinate web of things one wholeheartedly cares about constitutes an answer to the question of how to live. But we cannot infer from their wholeheartedness and their centrality to the agent that they are volitionally necessary in either a specieswide or a person-specific way. Or so I have averred. There may be a tendency, however, to make some such inference, a tendency grounded in a way of tying together volitional necessity and personal identity. A change in such basic commitments would be such a fundamental change, we might try to say, that the result is a different person. Such changes are not volitionally possible for the person, then, because the very same person could not begin and end in that way.[5]

This is not persuasive, however.[6] I do think it is important that such commitments normally help constitute and support the kinds of cross-temporal continuities and connections that a Lockean would see as central to personal identity over time. That is part of the reason why we find it natural to say that these commitments have authority to speak for the agent, that they constitute where that agent stands.[7] But a change in such commitments is, of course, not a way of dying.[8] So although there is a connection to personal identity, I don't think we can use it to support an inference from psychological centrality to volitional necessity.

Frankfurt thinks that our "mature confidence" is grounded "in what we cannot help being"—in our volitional necessities. My remarks so far point—albeit quite roughly and incompletely—to a somewhat different picture.

The basic idea is that your mature confidence in how you are living—and so your self-esteem and contentment—could be grounded, not primarily in volitional necessity, but rather in your thought that this is where you now stand, this is what you wholeheartedly care about, this helps organize your life, it has survived thoughtful reflection so far, and you now see no good reason to change and plenty of reason not to. It is in this sense settled for you. Although you have the capacity to change, you are confident that you will not change.[9]

Support for this stability may come in part from your recognition that changing what you already wholeheartedly care about, and so what now speaks for you, has an impact on the cross-temporal coherence and unity of your life, an impact that normally tends to frustrate things that you wholeheartedly care about—including concerns with the integrity of your life over time. This recognition will support a kind of conservatism: what you have already come to care about wholeheartedly will function as a kind of defeasible default. This is one way—to use Frankfurt's title—of taking oneself seriously. And this conservatism will be reasonable in the sense that it will be supported by what you wholeheartedly care about.

I wonder, then, whether some such reasonable, thoughtful stability of wholehearted caring can do much of the philosophical work that Frankfurt wants volitional necessity to do. Many of the things we wholeheartedly care about are, I suspect, things we could give up but are confident that we will not now give up because, when we take ourselves sufficiently seriously, we see no reason to make such a deep change in how we live, and plenty of reason not to. It is not clear to me why that is not enough for the authority of such carings to speak for us and establish where we stand, and for grounding the self-confidence and self-esteem that are Frankfurt's concern. Further, if this is enough for such authority, then we should ask whether, even in the case of person-specific volitionally necessary love, it is such thoughtful, reasonable stability, rather than incapacity, that is central to our mature confidence. After all, in the case of person-specific volitional necessities, we still may well have it in our power to take steps in the direction of future change. So we may still reflect on whether to do that.

Frankfurt's thought that our mature confidence is, rather, primarily grounded in "what we cannot help being" may overstate the parallels, with which he begins these wonderful lectures, between reason and the will. While reason involves a kind of necessity, the fundamental role of the will in our practical lives may be primarily a matter of a thoughtful, reasonable stability.

Socializing Harry

MEIR DAN-COHEN

To say that I agree with everything Harry Frankfurt said in his lectures understates the case, since as a matter of fact I acquired my views on these matters from him. Though I haven't been Harry's student, I read him early on and so at a susceptible age. There is little of a critical nature that I have to say. What I'd like to do instead is to consider some possible implications of Frankfurt's position on practices he did not explicitly address: those of holding people responsible, and relatedly of blaming and punishment. Extending Frankfurt's approach in this direction reveals additional power in it; to fully realize this power, however, Frankfurt's focus on individual psychology has to be expanded to take account of the intersubjective or the social. There are two main themes in the lectures, as there are in Frankfurt's work in general: one concerns freedom of the will and autonomy, and the second concerns the nature of normativity. They can be summarized as follows. First, we either identify with an attitude, or we don't. This defines the shape of the will, the extent of our autonomy, and, as he puts it elsewhere, the boundaries of the self. Second, we either care for something or we don't. This provides the ground of normativity. My general point can be best seen as a comment on the *we* in these statements. Frankfurt uses the pronoun distributively, whereas in extending the theory in the direction I propose, the "we" would better serve if used collectively.

I'll mostly refer to Lecture One, then comment more briefly on Lecture Two. Lecture One addresses the shape of the will and the nature of autonomy, but it treats also of responsibility, and as I said, my main interest is in the latter term. When are we responsible? What are we responsible for? In contemplating these questions, I find it helpful to consider a couple of legal cases, though I don't mean to make much of the cases' legal provenance; I use them for the most part just as actual recorded instances in which judgments of moral responsibility are made.

The key to Frankfurt's conception of autonomy, but also of responsibility, is of course the idea of identification. In his lectures, the connection between responsibility and identification is indicated most explicitly in the discussion of character. According to Frankfurt, responsibility for character "is not essentially a matter of *producing that character* but of *taking responsibility for it.* This happens when a person selectively identifies with certain of his own attitudes and dispositions, whether or not it was he that caused himself to have them. In identifying with them, he incorporates those attitudes and dispositions into himself and makes them his own" (7). It's a short step, I suppose, from this account of responsibility for the character traits themselves to a similar account of the responsibility the agent bears for actions that issue from those character traits and in which those traits are exhibited or expressed.

This extension of the theory of responsibility can be applied to a dramatic hypothetical that Frankfurt presents. Frankfurt imagines himself as a loving father who is beset by a desire to kill his son. "The desire," he says "is wildly exogenous; it comes entirely out of the blue," and it "is ordinarily safely repressed" (12). But now consider the harrowing situation in which the repression is unsuccessful and in which the desire does prevail. This in fact happened in the case of *Regina v. Charlson*.[1]

The defendant's ten-year-old son entered his father's study. With apparently no reason, Charlson hit the child over the head with a heavy mullet and threw him out of the window. Fortunately, the child was not killed. At his trial, Charlson successfully pleaded *involuntariness*: he was suspected of suffering of a brain tumor, and he alleged that that explained his behavior. A claim of involuntariness amounts to a total denial of responsibility equivalent to the statement, "I didn't really do it." Now on the conventional understanding of involuntariness, this claim is read with the stress on the word "do." The inquiry is: Was an action involved here? And this we tend to interpret as raising a further question of control: Could Charlson have acted otherwise? Was compliance with the law an option for him at the time?

The difficulty with this conventional interpretation can

be seen starkly if we compare *Charlson* with another case, *State v. Snowden*.[2] Snowden was involved in what appeared to be a minor quarrel with a woman outside a bar. At some point, he claimed at his trial, she kicked him. In response Snowden took out a knife and stabbed her to death, inflicting more than ninety wounds over her entire body. Snowden's explanation of this response was simple: when kicked by the victim, he flew into a rage; in his own words, "I blew my top." But, I think not surprisingly, Snowden's defense wasn't nearly as successful as Charlson's. He was convicted of first-degree murder.

Now when interpreted in terms of the idea of control, the difference in results is puzzling. Can it be said beyond reasonable doubt—which, after all, is the standard of proof in a criminal trial—that Snowden could have contained his temper, reined in his fury, and subdued his murderous impulse? Indeed, on Frankfurt's view this counterfactual inquiry is misguided. That a defendant may not have been able to act otherwise than he did, far from releasing him from responsibility, may actually be the ground of his responsibility. This would be the case were he impelled by *volitional necessity*, which is on Frankfurt's view the paradigm of free will and autonomy.

Frankfurt's approach suggests instead that we reorient the inquiry by reading the claim "I didn't really do it" implicitly made in these cases, with a different intonation, accenting the 'I.' Applied to Charlson, the claim is, "It was not really 'I' who brought about the injury, it was the tumor." In Frankfurt's terms, Charlson refuses to identify with whatever prompted his murderous outburst and to take responsibility for it. He "banishes" these promptings by placing them outside the boundaries of his self, or to reverse the metaphor, he draws his boundary so as to leave these promptings outside. Either way, the control such promptings exercise over Charlson is "external" and "tyrannical." This would explain why he was indeed acquitted. Frankfurt's approach also explains why we don't seem to be particularly perturbed by whether or not Snowden was able to contain his rage and subdue his outburst. On Frankfurt's view, the fact that Snowden couldn't help but act the way he did is, as far as his responsibility is concerned, neither here nor there.

The difficulty, however, is that as it stands Frankfurt's own account may exempt Snowden of responsibility. On this account, the maneuver attempted by Snowden closely resembles Charlson's. By saying that he blew his top, Snowden can be understood to convey his refusal to identify with this irresistible rage; like Charlson, he too would rather draw the boundary of his self in a way that leaves the fury outside. If such dissociation were successful, it would, after all, keep him, as it did Charlson, out of jail. But at least as far as the jury in this case was concerned, the maneuver failed. What are we to make of Charlson's success in defending himself against criminal charges and Snowden's corresponding failure?

The basic insight that greatly contributes to our understanding of these cases seems to me the connection indicated by Frankfurt between responsibility and the boundaries of self. But when it comes to the ascription of responsibility,

Frankfurt's approach must be supplemented in order to account for the difference between the two cases. The crucial point here is that the self's boundaries—what counts as a component of one's will or a trait of one's character—are not drawn unilaterally, not only from within. The shape of the self is at least in part the product of what we may call *constitutive practices*, including those of law and morality. Central among these practices are those of ascribing or withholding responsibility. As the cases seem to me to suggest, the drawing of the self's boundaries may involve a process of negotiation, in which the agent participates, but over which she has no unilateral control. Through the jury, society plays an active role in drawing the defendant's boundary. On this view, the verdict in *Snowden* amounts to a determination that rage is internal to the self; a regrettable yet legitimate component of one's character and personality; something for which one bears responsibility.

Although questions of responsibility arise on innumerable other occasions as well, the criminal trial provides a particularly visible and stylized setting for the kind of negotiation involved. The normative stakes in drawing the self's boundary are also particularly high in this context. Defendants are typically anxious to draw their boundary narrowly so as to escape the nasty ramifications of legal responsibility. This need not be just strategic posturing on their part: the phenomenology of withdrawal or flight from responsibility is altogether familiar and real. The prosecutor, eager to pin down responsibility to advance law enforcement and carry out justice, can be prompted by equally genuine indignation and resentment to advocate drawing the self's boundary widely. These momentary pressures and concerns of the trial should not, however, be allowed to eclipse the long-term and more general normative incidents of the self's boundary. The latter are obviously more complex than the immediate, momentary ones, but the political context from which the boundaries metaphor is drawn provides a useful, if simplified, analogy that affords a glimpse of the main considerations.

A state's boundary settles at once the scope of both its sovereignty and responsibilities. Replacing sovereignty with autonomy, the more apt label for an individual's self-rule, we get a picture in which autonomy and responsibility are coextensive, both defined by the boundaries of the self. To abdicate responsibility by contracting the self's boundary is accordingly also to forfeit part of one's autonomy, since by evacuating potential responsibility bases we also give up regions of autonomy and self-rule. Moreover, responsibility is itself a two-sided concept. The moral and especially the legal context focus for the most part on bad or forbidden behavior and thus bring to mind responsibility's negative side, as a source of blame and a basis for sanctions. But questions of responsibility also arise concerning credit due for positive actions and events. By defining the scope of one's responsibility, the boundaries of the self thus determine not only the extent of one's vulnerability to blame and punishment, but also the sources of satisfaction and gratification, of praise and reward.[3]

Drawing the self's boundary is accordingly, and not

surprisingly, a delicate and complicated balancing act, in which both the momentary and the long-term perspectives play a part, and in which conflicting considerations and difficult trade-offs apply. I will not expand any further these cursory remarks on the nature of this process and will instead briefly comment on the connection between the ascription of responsibility, which Frankfurt does not explicitly consider, and the assumption of responsibility, which he does. I do so by relating this connection to another, I think particularly moving, point in the lectures.

Frankfurt speaks of harmony within the self, a congruity between higher-order attitudes and lower-order ones, and links this state to Spinoza's ideal of "acquiescentia in se ipso," or "acquiescence to oneself." If the self's boundaries are drawn, as I suggest, through social practices, in the public domain, and in a process that involves something like a negotiation between the agent and others, another form of harmony or dissonance comes into view. The negotiation may end in agreement, as it apparently did in the *Charlson* case, where society, represented by the jury, came to accept the defendant's dissociative maneuver and drew the boundary accordingly. There is, however, the possibility of a breakdown in negotiations, with each party insisting on his or her own version as to where the borderline is drawn. *Snowden* may be such a case. I say may be, because more than one scenario may unfold. One possibility is for Snowden to persist in the face of the conviction in denying his responsibility. Either in proud defiance or in embittered self-pity, he'll consider himself the victim of two external forces that ruined his life: his rage is one, a cruel and uncomprehending jury the other. There is another possibility, however. Snowden may come to accept the verdict. This means that he will now align the boundary of his self as he conceives of it with society's. Contrition, atonement, and remorse are mechanisms through which such harmony between Snowden and society can be restored. A single version of his self, rather than two incompatible and competing versions, will emerge.

But what does it mean to speak about two competing versions of one and the same self? It may at first appear that there's got to be a fact of the matter as to where a thing's boundary lies. In a case of disagreement, one party—in our case, either Snowden or the jury—must have gotten it wrong. But this appearance is dispelled by the constitutive view of the process by which the boundary is drawn. Antecedent to the negotiations, there is no fact of the matter; the process fixes the segment of the boundary that is under dispute. It may be felt, however, that once the process is over and the boundary fixed one way or another, there can be only one self. Refusing to acknowledge it at this point amounts to ignoring the facts. It is an advantage of the metaphor we're using that it does not force this conclusion on us either. In the international arena from which the metaphor derives, indeterminacy in the drawing of borders is all too familiar. There need not exist a single authority whose judgment is accepted by all. Hence different and incompatible versions may persist, frequently with more or less disastrous consequences.

These further implications of applying to the self the idiom of boundaries seem to me altogether apt. The

possibility that the self's boundaries should be contested
and indeterminate, and that there should be more than one
version of a self, is altogether real. To entertain these possibilities and make sense of them, however, we cannot think
of the self as just a matter of psychological fact. The domain
to which this kind of contestation and indeterminacy
properly belongs and in which competing versions of one
and the same thing coexist is the domain of meaning and
interpretation. Ascriptions and assumptions of responsibility are *constitutive interpretations* of the self. And what makes
interpretations, hence competing interpretations, possible is
the self's intelligibility: that it's constituted by meaning.

I'm not sure whether Frankfurt will welcome or resist this
attempt to socialize his theory. Before we find out, I want
to briefly indicate the implications of the same attempt for
the second theme of his lecture, the issue of moral authority.
Here again my interest is in the kinds of practices that the
cases I've mentioned illustrate: not just ascribing responsibility, but blaming and punishing. Can Frankfurt's approach
account for these as well?

According to Frankfurt, the authority of morality, and
more broadly of all judgments of importance, is grounded
at bottom in what we care about; in "the attitudes and
dispositions of the individual" (23). "If what we should care
about depends upon what we do care about, any answer to
the normative question must be derived from considerations
that are manifestly subjective" (24). This view, I take it, parallels the one that was held by Bernard Williams, and in both
cases the implication is that to blame others is pointless in a

sense, unless they too care for what one cares about—unless their will is aligned in the relevant respect with one's own. But Frankfurt's view has the further and more striking implication that one can't really blame others even when their will is aligned with one's own. Surely my will has authority only over me. If the authority of morality derives from my will when my will endorses or accepts it, morality too has authority exclusively over me. By what right can I invoke its imperatives to blame others?

Put in other words, Frankfurt offers an attractive and metaphysically lean construal of the Kantian view that each person is a law unto himself. However, a question of jurisdiction now arises: even if the laws of two states have the same content, each state can prosecute only the violation of its own laws, not the other's, because each legal system has authority only domestically. According to Frankfurt, if I violate my deep values and convictions, I betray myself; and by the same token, if you violate your values and convictions, even if they resemble mine, you betray yourself. What business is this of mine, though? By what authority can I condemn you? Of course, I can be mad at you for harming me or the things I love, or disparage you for your hypocrisy or for the weakness of your will. But neither anger nor disparagement is the same as blame. To be able to blame you for the violation of a moral norm, we must be both under its jurisdiction. One and the same norm must have authority over both of us. Where would such authority come from?

It is my prerogative as commentator to raise questions without answering them, but my comments on Frankfurt's

first theme do indicate the general direction in which an
answer may be sought. On Frankfurt's view, the authority
of what's important comes from its importance for us. As
I noted at the outset, Frankfurt uses the "us" distributively,
whereas I propose to use it collectively. Support for this
suggestion can be found in another insightful observation
in Frankfurt's lecture: "The fact that there are things that we
do care about [or, to use Frankfurt's other expression, that
things are *important* to us] is plainly more basic to us—more
constitutive of our essential nature—than what those things
are" (19). What I take to be essential to human nature on
this view is that some things appear to us under a certain
description or designation, namely as "important." The point
as I understand it is that not only do some things appear as
"important to me," but also, and crucially, that certain things
appear to me as "important." *Important*, however, is a word,
specifically an adjective, and what it takes for something to be
important is that the adjective apply to it. But to say this is to
withdraw exclusive authority from the individual over this bit
of content or meaning. My suggestion is that taking ourselves seriously requires that we take seriously the semantics
of words, or the concepts, such as *important*, that according
to Frankfurt's own view play in human beings an essential,
constitutive role.

Once again, this is an appeal to an intersubjective context
and to our mutual intelligibility. Though we often disagree
vehemently about what is important, this is a disagreement
in our understanding and interpretation of a single term
or concept. All of us are willful subjects of one and the

same authority, the authority of important and kindred basic normative terms such as perhaps right or appropriate, whose meanings are embedded in a shared conceptual framework that secures our common human intelligibility. When we blame each other, we invoke this authority, under which we all live.[4] To use again the legal analogy, we are more like lawyers who disagree about the proper interpretation of one and the same statute whose authority they all concede than like the inhabitants of two different jurisdictions whose statutes happen to resemble each other.

Notes

TAKING OURSELVES SERIOUSLY

1. I will not discuss whether this needs to be modified to refer also to what we *would* care about if we were properly acquainted with it. In any case, the modification could readily be absorbed into the voluntaristic account of practical normativity that I am developing.

2. Thomas Nagel, *The Possibility of Altruism* (Oxford: Clarendon Press, 1970), 3.

3. If the modification mentioned in note 1 above is adopted, the pertinent question (concerning what the person *would* care about) will still be straightforwardly factual.

GETTING IT RIGHT

1. David Hume, *A Treatise of Human Nature*, ed. L. A. Selby-Bigge (Oxford: Oxford University Press, 1888), book 2, Part 3, section 3, p. 416 (emphasis added).

2. Robert M. Adams, *Finite and Infinite Goods* (Oxford: Oxford University Press, 1999), 18.

3. These quotations are from "Persons, Character, and Morality," in

Bernard Williams, *Moral Luck* (Cambridge: Cambridge University Press, 1981), 12–14.

4. J. Burnet, *Early Greek Philosophy* (London: A & C Black, 1948), 177 (fragment 13).

5. There may be similarly irreducible conflicts within a single person, for whom there will then be no alternatives but to separate one part of himself radically from the other or to endure tumultuous inner conflict.

6. It is worth noticing that Descartes found it impossible to rely confidently on theoretical reason without first acquiring—through his argument that God could not have made him so defective as to be misled by the clear and distinct perceptions that he could not help accepting—a firm confidence in the necessities of his own cognitive nature. My argument about the ground of practical normativity is, I believe, significantly analogous to his argument about the ground of theoretical reason.

MORALITY AND THE LOGIC OF CARING
Christine M. Korsgaard

1. I have argued for these views in Korsgaard, *The Sources of Normativity* (Cambridge: Cambridge University Press, 1996), esp. at §3.2.1–3.2.4, 92–100, and in "Fellow Creatures: Kantian Ethics and Our Duties to Animals," in *The Tanner Lectures on Human Values*, ed. Grethe B. Peterson (Salt Lake City: University of Utah Press, 2005), Vol. 25/26; and on the Internet at http://www.tannerlectures.utah.edu/.

2. Or, on Frankfurt's view, an agent may be committed to caring about morality because he cares about something to which morality is instrumental, or for which it is a necessary condition. The important issue, from my point of view, is whether we might be committed to morality simply by virtue of caring about something—I mean by caring about anything at all. Frankfurt denies that; he thinks that a commitment to morality depends on our particular concerns.

3. Despite what I say later in the text about self-consciousness plac-

ing us directly under the authority of reason, I think there is a sense in which it is true that particular instances of valuing are what commit us to reason and morality. Valuing anything whatever (or treating anything as a reason) commits us to morality, but it is possible, at least in theory, not to value anything or treat anything as a reason. See *Sources of Normativity*, §4.4.1–4.4.2, 160–64.

4. Frankfurt may be tempted to reply that he does not mean that caring involves a norm that you go on desiring; it is only that it includes a desire that you go on desiring. But I think he is committed to the norm because he is committed to thinking not only that you should go on desiring if you care, but that you should continue to care. That demand may derive from a yet higher order desire, in his scheme of things, but no matter—the demand will resound all the way back, and for Frankfurt, that's what a norm amounts to. In discussion, Frankfurt also admitted that one might be committed by caring about some contingent thing to also caring about one's wholeheartedness, freedom, and activity. The general idea is that someone who cares about anything also cares about caring, and so about the conditions that make caring and its exercise possible.

5. As I think of them, these commitments are grounded in what I call the "constitutive standards" of believing, or willing—or in Frankfurt's view, caring. The standards are constitutive of believing, or willing, or caring, because you do not count as believing, or willing, or caring unless you at least acknowledge the normative force of the commitments in question. Yet they are still normative standards, for it is possible to violate them; if it were not, they could not function as normative standards, which guide and correct agents who are tempted to violate them. Although as I argue in the text, willing the means is constitutive of willing the end, it still must be possible in some sense for an agent to will an end and fail to will the means, or Kant's hypothetical imperative could not function as a normative principle. (See my "The Normativity of Instrumental Reason," in *Ethics and Practical Reason*, ed. Garrett Cullity and Berys Gaut [Oxford: Clarendon Press, 1997].) Applying the model of

a constitutive standard to Frankfurt's notion of caring, I would say that it is possible for someone to care about something and yet violate the constitutive standards of caring, whatever they might be. Frankfurt clearly agrees with this, for in the passage I just quoted, he describes someone as failing to meet the standard that one must continue to desire what one cares about, and as correcting this "lapse" under the influence of that standard. Yet the standard of continuing to desire is constitutive of caring, for no one can care about something and at the same time openly reject that standard.

6. I am interested in this kind of argument, because in *The Sources of Normativity*, I tried to deploy an argument of this kind. I argued that an agent who values anything whatever is thereby committed to the value of humanity, and that a commitment to the value of humanity in turn implies a commitment to morality, most obviously in the form of Kant's Formula of Humanity as an End in Itself. In these comments, I will suggest somewhat different arguments for the same conclusion, which I believe come to the same thing in the end, although I won't try to explain that point here. Another argument with this structure is the famous argument in *Metaphysics* (IV.4 1006b10–15), in which Aristotle claims that a person is committed to the principle of noncontradiction just by virtue of making an assertion—any assertion whatever—and meaning something in particular by it. This is very like the view I am about to present in the text: that you are committed to universalizability just by virtue of willing something in particular—so to speak, by willing a maxim and meaning something in particular by it.

7. It places us under both the hypothetical and categorical imperatives at once because in order to serve as a law for the will, a maxim must describe a procedure that is both efficacious and universalizable. A similar argument, starting from the fact that we are aware of the grounds of our beliefs and can question them, should explain why we are directly under the authority of theoretical reason.

8. Frankfurt does not say whether he thinks something parallel about theoretical reason. I take it as a heuristic principle that we should

avoid positing disanalogies between theoretical and practical reason as far as possible—and if practical reason depended on love for its authority while theoretical reason did not, there would be a very striking disanalogy. The question here is whether there is a kind of theoretical reason that corresponds to Frankfurt's idea of volitional rationality. Here is one possibility: someone who supposes that his senses do not provide him with any evidence of what the world is like is not guilty of any formal contradiction or fallacy. But perhaps he might strike us as being lunatic or inhuman in the same way that someone who loves death or pain does.

9. Frankfurt argues that morality cannot be grounded in reason because "People who behave immorally incur a distinctive kind of opprobrium, which is quite unlike the normal attitude towards those who reason poorly." In my view, this is a good criticism of dogmatic rationalists like Samuel Clarke, Richard Price, W. D. Ross, and H. A. Prichard, but not of the views of Plato, Aristotle, or Kant—or for that matter of Nagel, who argues that the practically irrational person suffers from a kind of practical solipsism, not from mere error. In Kant's view, the role of the principles of reason is to unify a manifold into a certain sort of object. Theoretical reason unifies experience into a representation of the world that we can find our way around in, and practical reason unifies the self or the will. The "opprobrium" we accord to the immoral (or even the weak of will) comes from the difficulty of interacting with those who lack integrity—who do not have unified wills. Frankfurt will not accept this answer, or at least will think that it is incomplete, because he thinks that evil people can have integrity, or completely unified wills, but that is another argument. See Harry G. Frankfurt, *The Reasons of Love* (Princeton, N.J.: Princeton University Press, 2004), 98.

10. In "The Normativity of Instrumental Reason."

11. There seem to be two kinds of volitional rationality in Frankfurt's view. In the passage where he introduces the idea, Frankfurt affirms that a person is volitionally irrational if he cares about something that strikes the rest of us as "crazy," "lunatic," or "inhuman" to care about, such as the preference of Hume's exemplar for the destruction of the world over

the scratching of his finger (29). But Frankfurt also seems to think that a
person is volitionally irrational if he acts against the things he loves, the
things he cannot help caring about, whatever those might be. It seems
odd to lump these two forms of "irrationality" together, because the
judgment that the first person is irrational is completely external to the
person himself—he does not resist his own necessities, but rather those
acknowledged by the rest of us. The other kind of volitional irrationality,
by contrast, involves the violation of one's own deepest will. It is hard to
see why the first kind of condition should be called "irrationality" at all.

12. Frankfurt thinks the unity of the will has two components:
freedom of the will, which gives us synchronic unity, and caring, which
provides diachronic unity. Freedom, as he understands it, just consists in
the fact that my second-order desires and any further orders of desire I
might have support the desire upon which I actually act at this moment.
I am synchronically unified because of lack of synchronic conflict. (A
wanton is also synchronically unified, I suppose, but only in a trivial
sense.) Caring, Frankfurt claims, motivates us to play an active role in
keeping our wills unified over time. On the Kantian view, there is no
need to appeal to these two separate components in order to secure
either unity or freedom. I have not performed an act of will even at this
moment unless I have made the potentially diachronic commitment to
willing my maxim as a universal law. My capacity to be unified even now
depends on my capacity to unify myself over time; and my freedom—my
autonomy—consists in the fact that my actions are governed by a law I
give to myself. So freedom, synchronic unity, and diachronic unity are
really all one thing.

13. Formal universalizability by itself seems to allow one to universalize over "all males," "all white people," "all Americans," or whatever. In the
text, I argue that what it cannot coherently do is universalize over "all
states of me."

14. Because I am testing a maxim of stealing an object, we may
assume that it is my end to possess the object. I am also assuming here
that the desire to possess the object that motivates my stealing it is not

merely a desire to possess it momentarily—to watch it pass through my hands, so to speak—but rather to have it at my disposal, over some period of time. On the importance of this condition for generating contradictions under the universal law test, see my "Kant's Formula of Universal Law," in *Creating the Kingdom of Ends* (New York: Cambridge University Press, 1996), esp. 98ff.

15. This question arises because you might be tempted to suppose that the Kantian route to morality that I have sketched above—from the commitment to the formal universality that is essential to the exercise of the will to the kind of universalizability needed for morality—is blocked by the failure of one of these two conditions. You might suppose that in order to constitute myself as something's cause, I need only universalize over all present and future instances of myself, or that the reasons that result from the formal universalizability requirement are only private reasons. If the inference from formal universalizability to morality fails in the first way, we are left with first-person egoism. If it fails in the second way, we are left with ethical egoism.

16. Why must the various conscious subjects of my body cooperate at all? On the argument I am now making, one answer that is not open to me is "because they are all me." For according to my argument, my continuing personal identity depends on whether I establish the unity of my will by willing universally. In his political philosophy, Kant argued that cooperation is morally required among agents who must share a geographical territory and therefore are likely to have conflicts of right about how to use it; although it sounds a little startling, it is tempting to regard the sharing of a body in a similar way.

A second and easier question is why it is not enough to suppose cooperation must take place between the conscious subject of my body at the time of making the appointment and the conscious subject of my body at the time of keeping it. The answer is that the intervening conscious subjects of my body must get my body to the dentist on time for the appointment, and more generally must act in a way that makes keeping the appointment possible.

17. One possible way to argue for this point is to argue that we require the cooperation of all causes—all of nature—in order to realize any one of our ends. Nature works as a system, and my efficacy as an agent in fact depends on the entire system cooperating with me. But I cannot address my law to all of nature, because as far as I know, the nonhuman part of nature isn't capable of conforming to a law. So instead I address it to all rational agents, all causes that are, in the eighteenth-century phrase, "capable of a law." I believe that our need to secure the cooperation even of the nonhuman part of nature in order to conceive ourselves as agents—that is, as in control of our effects—is behind Kant's philosophy of religion, especially as presented in the dialectic of the *Critique of Practical Reason* (trans. Mary Gregor; Cambridge: Cambridge University Press, 1997).

18. For another statement of this argument, see what is now Lecture Six of my Locke Lectures, *Self-Constitution: Agency, Identity, and Integrity*, forthcoming from Oxford University Press.

19. I think that we can also explain why accepting the logical implications of proposition P is constitutive of accepting P, if we can explain why the basic principles of logic are constitutive of believing, which I think is also possible. For one step in such an explanation, see "The Normativity of Instrumental Reason," 248.

20. See my "Self-Constitution in the Ethics of Plato and Kant," *The Journal of Ethics* 3 (1999): 1–29.

21. For more on this last claim, see my "Acting for a Reason," in *Studies in Practical Reason*, ed. Bradley Lewis (Washington DC: Catholic University Press, forthcoming).

22. See my "Fellow Creatures."

23. In his part of *Utilitarianism For and Against*, and also in "Persons, Character, and Morality." I have also heard Williams, in conversation, criticize it for being based on "empirical studies that are not forthcoming," because no one has ever actually tried to prove that the utilities work out this way.

24. A number of different solutions have been proposed, most

notably Thomas Nagel's attempt to separate agent-relative and agent-neutral reasons in *The View from Nowhere* (New York: Oxford University Press, 1986), and Samuel Scheffler's idea of an "agent-centered prerogative" in *The Rejection of Consequentialism* (Oxford: Clarendon Press, 1982).

25. This is suggested by what Frankfurt says about value in *The Reasons of Love*, 56.

26. T. M. Scanlon, *What We Owe to Each Other* (Cambridge, Mass.: Harvard University Press, 1998), 164–65.

27. This is consistent with thinking, as I do, that all values arise originally from acts of valuing by individual agents. I just have to think that another's right to her organs arises from her own self-concern, which I must acknowledge as a source of reasons, and not from my concern for her. In another kind of case, where the value is not that of a person or animal, it may be because I am inclined to make this my project that I think of it as having universal or intersubjective value. On my view, every rational being is, in a way, entitled to create value through his interests. Philosophy, for instance, is intersubjectively valuable in the first instance because there are some human beings who want to think things through, and choose to do so. Yet once it is established as a valuable thing, my desire to stand in a special relationship to it is still something different.

28. In "The Reasons We Can Share," in Korsgaard, *Creating the Kingdom of Ends* (New York: Cambridge University Press, 1996), 275–310; see especially the discussion at 284–91.

29. Frankfurt thinks that the reason we want the things we love to be of value is that "love commits us to significant requirements and limitations" (43). I think there is more to it than that. It is not just that if you love something or someone, you are going to take trouble over it or him. It is that love essentially wants a worthy object, even though it is not caused by the perception of value. I have described one view of why this might be so in "The General Point of View: Love and Moral Approval in Hume's Ethics," in *Hume Studies* 25 (April–November 1999): 1–39.

Putting together the two arguments in these comments: it cannot make sense for me to care about writing my book so much that I am willing to endanger the health of the Africans in order to write it because the reasons I am deriving from my commitment to the book's value would be ones the Africans could not possibly share with me.

30. In terms of the argument of The Sources of Normativity, part of what I have in mind here is this: when you come to see that your contingent practical identities are normative for you only insofar as they are endorsable from the point of view of your human identity, you also come to have a new attitude toward the personal projects embodied in those contingent practical identities. You come to see them as various realizations of human possibility and human value, and to see your own life that way. Your life fits into the general human story and is a part of the general human activity of the creation and pursuit of value. It matters to you both that it is a particular part—your own part—and that it is a part of the larger human story. (This is the attitude that I think Marx may have in mind when he talks about "species being.") In the third part of A Theory of Justice (Cambridge, Mass.: Harvard University Press, 1971), Rawls argues that citizenship in a just society fosters an attitude of vicarious participation of the citizens in each others' activities, so that they see themselves as members of a community with a common culture in which they each do their part. I am suggesting that membership in the Kingdom of Ends makes us regard ourselves as parts of a common humanity in the same way.

A THOUGHTFUL AND REASONABLE STABILITY
Michael E. Bratman

Many thanks to Gideon Yaffe for helpful comments on an earlier draft. This essay was written while I was a fellow at the Center for Advanced Study in Behavioral Sciences. I am grateful for financial support provided by the Andrew W. Mellon Foundation.

1. I take it that such love is not merely a minimally benevolent concern—as when, in Hume's example, you avoid, at no personal cost, someone else's gouty toes.

2. Harry G. Frankfurt, *The Reasons of Love* (Princeton, N.J.: Princeton University Press, 2004), 98.

3. Because Frankfurt indicates that he rejects normative realism (32–33), it is worth noting that an expressivist metaethics can also seek to make sense of this critical thought.

4. Frankfurt, *The Reasons of Love*, 98.

5. An argument very roughly like this seems to be suggested by Frankfurt in his "Autonomy, Necessity, and Love," in *Necessity, Volition, and Love* (Cambridge: Cambridge University Press, 1999), 129–41, at 139.

6. See J. David Velleman, "Identification and Identity," in S. Buss and L. Overton, eds., *Contours of Agency: Essays on Themes from Harry Frankfurt* (Cambridge, Mass.: MIT Press, 2002), 91–123.

7. Or so I maintain in my "Reflection, Planning, and Temporally Extended Agency," *Philosophical Review* 109 (2000): 35–61.

8. As Velleman emphasizes in "Identification and Identity," at 98–99; and as Frankfurt acknowledges in his "Reply to J. David Velleman," in Buss and Overton, *Contours of Agency*, 124–28, at 124–25 and n1.

9. Perhaps you see no good reason even to reassess because you are fully confident that further reflection would not change things. This is a thought that Frankfurt once appealed to when he compared practical decision to deciding to trust one's earlier calculations, because one expects one would get the same answer if one did it again. See his "Identification and Wholeheartedness," in *The Importance of What We Care About* (Cambridge: Cambridge University Press, 1988), 159–76, at 167–69. Nadeem Hussain appeals to a related idea in his "Practical Reflection and Reasons" (unpublished manuscript).

SOCIALIZING HARRY
Meir Dan-Cohen

1. *Regina v. Charlson*, I W.L.R. at 317 (1955).

2. *State v. Snowden*, 79 Idaho 266, 313 P.2d 706 (1957). For a more complete discussion of some of the issues regarding responsibility raised by the

juxtaposition of these two cases and related matters, see my "Responsibility and the Boundaries of the Self," *Harvard Law Review* 105 (1992); a revised version appears as chapter 7 in *Harmful Thoughts: Essays on Law, Self and Morality*, (Princeton: Princeton University Press, 2002).

3. This is obviously a close variant of the trade-offs associated with the Stoic way of life.

4. This is not to imply any prospect of general agreement on what counts as important; and blaming should of course be sensitive to the inevitability and legitimacy of differences of opinion. But this picture also leaves logical room for blaming by invoking a common authority and one's honest, if contested, interpretation of its relevant implications.

Index